PRAISE FOR THE SETH BOOKS

"The Seth books present an alternate map of reality with a new diagram of the psyche . . . useful to all explorers of consciousness."
— Deepak Chopra, author of *The Seven Spiritual Laws of Success*

"Seth was one of my first metaphysical teachers. He remains a constant source of knowledge and inspiration in my life."
— Marianne Williamson, author of *A Return to Love*

"I would like to see the Seth books as required reading for anyone on their spiritual pathway. The amazing in-depth information in the Seth books is as relevant today as it was in the early '70s when Jane Roberts first channeled this material."
— Louise Hay, author of *You Can Heal Your Life*

"Seth's teachings had an important influence on my life and work, and provided one of the initial inspirations for writing *Creative Visualization*."
— Shakti Gawain, author of *Creative Visualization*

"The Seth books were of great benefit to me on my spiritual journey and helped me to see another way of looking at the world."
— Gerald G. Jampolsky, author of *Love is Letting Go of Fear*

"As you read Seth's words, you will gain more than just new ideas. Seth's energy comes through every page — energy that expands your consciousness and changes your thoughts about the nature of reality."
— Sanaya Roman, author of *Living with Joy*

"Quite simply one of the best books I've ever read."
— Richard Bach, author of *Jonathan Livingston Seagull*

"To my great surprise — and slight annoyance — I found that Seth eloquently and lucidly articulated a view of reality that I had arrived at only after great effort and an extensive study of both paranormal phenomena and quantum physics. . . ."
— Michael Talbot, author of *The Holographic Universe*

BOOKS BY JANE ROBERTS

The Rebellers (1963)

The Coming of Seth (How to Develop Your ESP Power) (1966)

The Seth Material (1970)

Seth Speaks: The Eternal Validity of the Soul, A Seth Book (1972)

The Education of Oversoul Seven (1973)

The Nature of Personal Reality, A Seth Book (1974)

Adventures in Consciousness (1975)

Dialogues of The Soul and Mortal Self in Time (1975)

Psychic Politics: An Aspect Psychology Book (1976)

The World View of Paul Cézanne: A Psychic Interpretation (1977)

The Afterdeath Journal of an American Philosopher: The World View of William James (1978)

The "Unknown" Reality: Vol. 1, A Seth Book (1977)

The "Unknown" Reality: Vol. 2, A Seth Book (1979)

The Further Education of Oversoul Seven (1979)

Emir's Education in the Proper Use of Magical Powers (1979)

The Nature of the Psyche: Its Human Expression, A Seth Book (1979)

The Individual and the Nature of Mass Events, A Seth Book (1981)

The God of Jane: A Psychic Manifesto (1981)

If We Live Again: Or, Public Magic and Private Love (1982)

Oversoul Seven and the Museum of Time (1984)

Dreams, "Evolution," & Value Fulfillment: Vol. 1, A Seth Book (1986)

Dreams, "Evolution," & Value Fulfillment: Vol. 2, A Seth Book (1986)

Seth, Dreams, and Projection of Consciousness (1986)

The Magical Approach, A Seth Book (1995)

The Way Toward Health, A Seth Book (1997)

A
Seth
BOOK

THE MAGICAL APPROACH

APPROACH

SETH SPEAKS ABOUT THE
ART OF CREATIVE LIVING

Jane Roberts

NOTES BY ROBERT F. BUTTS

AMBER-ALLEN PUBLISHING

NEW WORLD LIBRARY
NOVATO, CALIFORNIA

Co-published by Amber-Allen Publishing and New World Library

EDITORIAL OFFICE:
Amber-Allen Publishing
P.O. Box 6657
San Rafael, CA 94903

DISTRIBUTION OFFICE:
New World Library
14 Pamaron Way
Novato, CA 94949

Editorial: Janet Mills
Cover Art: Robert F. Butts
Cover Design: Beth Hansen

Library of Congress Cataloging-in-Publication Data

Seth, (Spirit), 1929–1984
   The magical approach : Seth speaks about the art of creative living / [channeled by] Jane Roberts ; notes by Robert F. Butts.
      p.   cm. – (A Seth book)
      "An Amber-Allen book"
      1. Spirit writings. 2. Self actualization (Psychology)–Miscellanea.
   I. Roberts, Jane, 1929–1984   II. Butts, Robert F.   III. Title.
   IV. Series: Seth (Spirit), 1929–1984. Seth book.
   BF1301.S377   1994   94 - 22091
   133.9'3–dc20   CIP

ISBN 978-1-878424-09-9
Printed in Canada

30   29   28   27   26   25   24

This book is dedicated
to
Jane Roberts Butts

May 8, 1929 – September 5, 1984

CONTENTS

MAGIC SHOW

What magicians we all are,
turning darkness into light,
transforming invisible atoms
into the dazzling theater
of the world,
pulling objects,
(people as well
as rabbits)
out of secret
microscopic closets,
turning winter into summer,
making a palmful of moments
disappear through time's trap door.

We learned the methods
so long ago
that they're unconscious,
and we've hypnotized ourselves
into believing
that we're the audience,
so I wonder where we served
our apprenticeship.
Under what master magicians did we learn
to form reality
so smoothly that we forgot to tell ourselves
the secret?

Jane Roberts, 1979

FOREWORD

My wife, Jane Roberts, dictated *The Magical Approach* for Seth, the "energy personality essence" she spoke for in a trance state, in 1980—but the pressures of Jane's illness, and of our producing other books, kept us from publishing it quickly. Then Jane died in 1984, at the age of 55. I was 65. Looking back from my position within the framework of simultaneous time, I'm amazed to see that another ten years passed before the publication of this little book by Amber-Allen/New World Library. Why the delay? What happened? Janet Mills, the publisher and editor for the new editions of Jane's books, suggested that I write a bit about the situation. Many others have asked over the years, and I'm very grateful for every one of those caring questions.

I know what happened, and yet consciously I'll never grasp all of the psychic ramifications involved. The day after Jane died I went back to work, finishing the last two Seth books to meet long-overdue publishing deadlines. Jane's and my dear friend, Debbie Harris, began making copies of all of the Seth sessions, plus the transcripts of Jane's ESP classes, for the "collection" of Jane's and my work in the archives of Yale University Library. But while I kept myself busy, and presented a smiling face to the world, I was numb inside. I cried for my wife several times a day for a year. Even though it's simultaneous, according to Seth, I needed "time" for my long journey of recovery.

Jane and I had corresponded with Laurel Lee Davies for several years. Five months after my wife's death, I called Laurel, who was an administrative assistant at a center for the arts and humanities in Los Angeles, California, for the first time. As the many hours of our calls quickly accumulated, Laurel and I came to understand through dreams that we had shared reincarnational relationships. In August of that year — 1985 — she moved to Elmira to work with me in a number of ways. She helped me carry on the massive project of continuing the work that Debbie Harris had begun: copying many more of the thousands of pages of Jane's and my work for the archives of the library at Yale. She answered mail, and put together a mailing list. She helped me proofread *Seth, Dreams, and Projection of Consciousness* for Stillpoint Publishing. Later, she helped me proofread the new editions of *Seth Speaks* and *The Nature of Personal Reality* that Amber-Allen/ New World Library has published. She's worked as a researcher of Jane's material for *The Magical Approach* — the book she has "most dreamed of working on." Laurel has been Seth's "metaphysical apprentice," as she recently put it, for fourteen years now. Even with our differences, our supportive and complicated relationship continues. Yet even so, as the years passed I began to better see that recovery from Jane's death was going to take the rest of my life; and that within the framework of simultaneous time uncounted millions of others had experienced that truth, were doing so now, and would be doing so. Maybe some day I'll write in detail about Jane's and my lives — but not now!

Other than a few close friends — Sue Watkins among them — I saw few people. Sue is mentioned in *The Magical Approach*. So is Tam Mossman, Jane's editor at Prentice-Hall. Tam was a great help in a number of ways. Beginning with the Spring 1985 issue, Tam published his very interesting quarterly, *Metapsychology: The Journal of Discarnate Intelligence,* for several years. He included Seth material in many issues. In the meantime I'd gone back to painting, which I'd given up for the last two years of Jane's life. I painted portraits of her as I met her in my dreams. I did no writing except for the "grief notebooks" that I composed about Jane's passing and my reactions to that event. Deliberate therapy, some of that.

Our beloved books began to go out of print, one by one, as sales slowly declined. I thought the letters from readers would also slack off. They did to some extent — but to my surprise and pleasure they continued to arrive at that slower but steady pace. I tried hard to answer each one of them. (I still do, although at this writing I'm far behind. I've let answering any but immediate business mail go while Laurel and I worked on the manuscript for *The Magical Approach.*)

For several years after Jane's death, I explored possible publishing ventures with old and trusted friends — people who, like Richard Kendall and Suzanne Delisle, sincerely wanted to see Jane's and my work kept in print. Richard had been a member of Jane's ESP class in the 1970s. Following her passing, as a paralegal he was also a great help in resolving some old and troublesome publishing hassles. At the same time, I wondered often if it was of any use to try publishing Seth books, old or new — why do so, if sales were falling? Maybe people were tired of the Seth material. Maybe Jane and I had already offered the best we could, for whatever our efforts were worth. The world would certainly go on, regardless.

Our books continued to go out of print, and in 1990 I began working with Anne Marie O'Farrell, a literary agent. She's married to Rick Stack, a writer, publisher, and lecturer involving things psychic; he too was a member of ESP class. Without Anne Marie's untiring help, I question whether I'd still be in publishing. For she "found" Janet Mills and Amber-Allen/New World Library. Like Laurel, both women are passionately interested in keeping Jane's work in print. Janet told me, after publishing the first two reprints, that she "would like to publish all of the books at once." And added that she was already getting requests to do just that.

In 1993, I saw the culmination of three ventures that I'd been involved in for varying periods of time: Lynda Dahl and Stan Ulkowski, of Seth Network International, published the first quarterly issue of the newly expanded Seth-oriented magazine, *Reality Change.* (*RC,* as everyone calls it, was founded by Maude Cardwell in June 1980; she began it as a two-page mimeographed newsletter.) Richard Roberts, of Vernal Equinox Press, published *A Seth Reader,* a volume consisting of excerpts from six of the Seth books. And Bob Terrio, of Bob Terrio Productions, marketed a video, *The Seth Phenomena,* in which I discuss Jane's and my work.

I'm still not finished with the duplication of Jane's and my papers for Yale University Library. Indeed, that long-range endeavor doesn't have to have a discrete end. I've learned that there will always be more to add to the collection.

For some time now Rick Stack and I have discussed a most intriguing project: the private printing, by Rick, of the complete transcripts of those first 510 sessions that Jane held before the publication of *The Seth Material* in 1970. This will be a massive job. The set of eight volumes will be called *The Early Sessions*, and will be sold by subscription only, at least in the beginning.

Sue Watkins, who described Jane's ESP class so well in her two-volume *Conversations with Seth*, recently began doing research for *Conversations with Jane Roberts: A Multidimensional Memoir.*

I'm very fortunate that the help of all of those I've mentioned, and of others, too, is enabling me to keep the promise I made to Jane on her deathbed ten years ago, when she asked me to publish all of her work. I know that my wife lives within me now, as I do within her "where she is now" — just as we shared ourselves with each other throughout the nearly twenty-nine years of our marriage. That simultaneous time passed with unbelievable depth and swiftness.

Life goes on, then, only it's different. Of course my feelings, while being unique in that they're my own, are intimately bound up with those of everyone else. How could it be otherwise, since no one can live in true isolation? Each one of us is an immortal portion, a spark of endless perception and beauty and feeling — and yes, of conflict and denial at times — within this probable reality that we're all creating together, even when we don't know we're doing it! I watch with awe as within this reality each one of us expresses as best we can our creative understanding of this wonderful mystery.

Robert F. Butts
November 19, 1994

INTRODUCTION

A DAY IN WHICH MAGIC COMES TO LIFE AND SETH DESCRIBES
WHAT "THE MAGICAL APPROACH" TO LIFE IS

BY JANE ROBERTS

Twice a week when evening comes (as most of my readers know) while our neighbors go to movies, or shopping plazas, or just have friends in to watch television, I go into a trance,[1] "become" Seth, and take on a kind of a second life, or a life within a life. Actually, the sessions usually last anywhere from one to three hours, so I suppose that many people spend a good deal more time than that playing golf or tennis.

In our case though, Rob and I usually have no direct audience (not that we can see anyhow), and those few hours spent in trance have an impact on my husband and me — and upon the world — out of context with the actual time expended.

As Seth I've produced five previous books: *Seth Speaks; The Nature of Personal Reality; The "Unknown" Reality, Volumes I and II; The Nature of the Psyche;* and *The Individual and the Nature of Mass Events*, and Seth is halfway through a sixth book: *Dreams, "Evolution," and Value Fulfillment*. These beside my own twelve books. Seth doesn't answer mail though, or do any typing, and so as a result of those trance hours Rob and I spend a good deal of our conscious energy dealing one way or another with the effects of that trance life.

In the summer of 1980 I missed Seth sessions for nearly two months. I was finishing work on one of my own books, *The God of Jane*. Rob was preparing Seth's *The Individual and the Nature of Mass Events* for publication. We were both caught up in the same events as most other people were during that June and July — the hotter-than-usual nights and days, the drought in parts of New York State that touched our area lightly, the TV news drama as the political parties argued and planned for their conventions. Some nights the (singing) bugs in the small back woods were louder than the sound of our television set. The same heat that made me groan with dismay turned Rob into some version of a south-sea island native. He looked supercool in his cut-off denim shorts; his long hair curled into natural corkscrews, his light durable frame seeming to luxuriate in the heat while my light durable frame turned into a sponge that added ten pounds of fatigue.

I was between projects after *The God of Jane*. In the meantime I'd read over the 17 chapters of my unfinished novel, *Oversoul Seven and the Museum of Time*, and looked over groups of notes for possible books, but nothing hit the spot. I asked for some ideas from my "natural spontaneous self," and on August 5, 1980, I dreamed that a moving van with me in it was itself being moved by a larger vehicle ahead of some planned time. There was a squabble over seating arrangements which was finally resolved. I took that to mean that I would shortly be on the move again creatively, and to be prepared, so I had Rob help me move all my writing materials from the small breezeway where I'd finished *The God of Jane*, into the new patio back room, as a gesture of being ready to start over.

So on August 6th I sat in the patio-room with fresh paper, fresh typewriter cartridge, and hopefully fresh mind, looking over my interpretations of Rob's latest dreams. It was a very hot August afternoon. The pieces of the world fell neatly into their proper places. The pictures of the moments clicked together as they usually do, each instant precise, yet leading into another. The motion seemed to be all exterior, from the too-warm wind that blew into my small studio from the back hill, to the shadows of moving foliage outside that flickered across the floor.

I was glancing at one of several pages of notes that Rob had written. At the lunch table I had remarked that a particular correspondent of ours wanted "instant magic," and my comment led to Rob writing some notes. As I started to read these notes at random this particular portion caught my attention . . . Rob wrote:

> Magic as we call it represents (reflects) a basic part of our natural heritage . . . We permit distorted versions of the psyche's attributes — clairvoyant, telepathic, and precognitive abilities — which surface as magic. [2]

Something in his words struck me in a new fashion. Rob and I often discussed such subjects. He was saying that we were immersed in "magic" no matter what we called it, that manifestations of telepathy, and so forth, were just places where our magic "showed." For some reason as I finished reading . . . I felt inspired. Or rather, I felt an inner psychological motion happening — a movement as definite, yet subtle as the shadows that flickered on the floor. A change of balance — a vital but usually-hidden psychic action that instantly changed me and the afternoon.

As I recognized the feeling of inspiration, I glanced idly to-ward the kitchen. The sight of the table struck my fancy, plus my view of the front doorway, with the green foliage showing through the open threshold. I thought about doing another painting of the scene; I hadn't done any painting in months. Then I thought of asking Rob to take a snapshot of the table area, so that I could paint it later. Not two minutes passed before Rob stood at my door with his camera! He'd bought a flash gadget several months ago to use with it, and he hadn't tried it out yet. Now he told me he had one exposure left, and he wanted to take a snapshot of me to use it up.

He had been fussing with the camera at the other end of the house from the den. There was no way, I thought, that I could have picked up physical clues as to his activity. Yet here he stood, camera and all.

My feelings "clicked;" the incident was significant; and it seemed to fit in too perfectly and meaningfully into the events just previous, as if saying "yes, you do operate magically" . . . and this is an example of how those perceptions work. If Rob hadn't come in at that point, I wouldn't have known that my thought about cameras had anything to do with his thoughts or activities at the same time. So how often do our thoughts relate in one way or another to the thoughts of others?[3]

I told Rob what I'd been thinking just before he came in. My hunch is that because of my state of mind — interpreting Rob's dreams, and my reading of his notes, I was in a particular kind of correspondence with him, or with his state of mind, that facilitat-ed the inner communication. We talked about it.

Suddenly I had a whole bunch of thoughts that I wanted to write up regarding this . . . "magical orientation" Rob was speaking of. Seth's "Framework 2" would be this magical area, of course, I thought. Yet except for the beginning of that (part) of Seth's material. Framework 2^4 never really got through to me emotionally. Somehow Rob's few notes did, or maybe I was just ready. The magical orientation to reality would include intellectual activity. That went without saying, but the way of relating to life would be completely different too; the way of dealing with problems or health difficulties; of achieving goals and so forth would be <u>drastically</u> different. The word "action" would mean something else than it does, too.

Rob's notes helped me realize that all of this wasn't as alien as it usually seems. The magical orientation might be in direct conflict with our training in this and most present cultures. But it would be part of our natural way of looking at the world — a way that has been overlaid by our belief in the "rational" way of doing things. That way was proving to be not so rational at all, incidentally. But I thought there would be things in each person's life that could be used as guideposts, to a magical kind of orientation. . . .

I took the fan into the bedroom, the coolest room in the house, sat down on the edge of the bed, and began to write down my own feelings about Rob's notes (and) the camera affair — and what I called the Magical Connection.

Heat or no, I had to notice that the room seemed plunged into greenness — the leaves trembling and the fir tree so close to the window that a branch could grow in if you left the window open long enough.

As I wrote the fan whirred, stirring the air against my skin as the green leaves winked — and I felt a trance at last entering the neighborhood of my mind. Seth, I knew, would start up the sessions again that night — if I wanted to. . . .[5]

I grinned. I wanted to. Yet after the two-month layoff I was nervous too; as I always was after any extended "trance vacation." Suppose — just suppose — I couldn't start up again or I lost the knack as suddenly as I'd acquired it (17 years before)? Or Seth spoke gibberish? I didn't really worry that such things might happen, but I was uneasily aware that they could. "Nonsense," I muttered, "it's the heat!" Because I knew that Seth would speak about the magical "connection." I managed another grin — and who should know more about "magic" than Seth? Didn't he emerge magically to begin with?

Around 4:00 the temperature hit 92 degrees and I thought of putting the session off. Rob and I took an hour's nap, though, and ate supper at the coffee table while watching the evening news. I wiggled around a lot trying to get comfortable while the "cool as a cucumber" Rob said what a great day it was. And finally, just after 8:30 I began to feel Seth around.

It was okay. After the layoff, there was Seth poised psychologically once again (for over the thousandth time). At the threshold of my mind those "psychic gears" turned. Rob was ready with his notebook and pen. I took a sip of my wine and ice. The fan whirred. A slightly cool breeze came in through the open doors and windows. Then I took off my glasses, "turned into" Seth, and began to speak. Bare legs propped up on the coffee table Rob sat, pen poised, and the session started.

※　※　※

Notes: Introduction by Jane Roberts

1. Jane Roberts writes in *The God of Jane:* "Since late 1963, I've clocked approximately 4,000 hours of trancetime, during which the Seth sessions have been held twice weekly. . . . My trancetime is more concentrated than regular time. I'm not unconscious but conscious in a different way, at another level . . . This state of perception has nothing to do with classical pathological dissociation; and its products — Seth's five books — display a highly-developed intellect at work and give evidence of a special kind of creativity. In those trance hours I 'turn into someone else.' At least I am not myself to myself; I become Seth, or a part of what Seth is. I don't feel 'possessed' or 'invaded' during sessions. I don't feel that some superspirit has 'taken over' my body. Instead it's as if I'm practicing some precise psychological art, one that is ancient and poorly understood in our culture; or as if I'm learning a psychological science that helps me map the contours of consciousness itself . . . after all this time, I'm finally examining the trance view of reality and comparing it to the official views of science and religion. . . .

"This is almost always an exhilarating experience, like riding some perfect gigantic ninth wave of energy, knowing exactly how and when to 'jump in', and feeling absolutely safe and supported even when embarked upon such a strange psychological flight. But the energy and power of *this* wave carries me above and below usual reality, sweeping me into contrasts that are microscopic and macroscopic by turns."

2. See Note 2 for Session Two.

3. See Appendix A for Jane's material on how some of her own thoughts "relate in one way or another to the thoughts of others." Included also are excerpts from Seth's material on a different prediction experience of Jane's.

4. In Note 2 for Session One, I quote myself and Seth on Frameworks 1 and 2.

5. See Rob's painting of Jane on the following page.

Robert F. Butts (1919–): *Jane Roberts.* 1969. Oil on panel, $12\frac{1}{2}$ x 10 in.

Jane had been speaking for Seth for six years when she posed for me. I don't regard my unsigned effort as being a finished work. It was just the best I could do at the time.

SESSION ONE

ASSEMBLY-LINE TIME VERSUS NATURAL, CREATIVE TIME.
THE RATIONAL MIND VERSUS THE ARTISTIC MIND.

AUGUST 6, 1980
8:48 P.M., WEDNESDAY

Good evening.

(*"Good evening, Seth."*)

Now: We will, as always, begin in our own way.

In your latest series of interworkings, you and Ruburt,[1] with your dreams and so forth, with Ruburt's notes and your own, were both heading in the proper direction, dealing with issues that are important personally, and that also have a much broader impact.

The natural person is indeed the <u>magical</u> person, and you have both to some extent had very recent examples of such activity. You were, and are, trying to teach yourselves something. This is somewhat lengthy to unravel, but your behavior and experience, of course, is the result of your beliefs. Framework 2^2 has been a rather fascinating but <u>mainly</u> (underlined) hypothetical framework, in that neither of you have really been able to put it to any perceivable use in your terms. This is not to say it has not been operating. You have not had the kind of feedback, however, that you want.

When you were both intensely involved in your projects, just finished, you let much of your inner experience slide, relatively speaking. The two of you operating together, however, then came up with an idea — an important one — that allows you to interpret the Framework 2 material in your own ways. You had instant feedback — the interplay of a creative nature between the two of you involving your dreams and the camera,[3] and so forth. You were each struck by the magical ease with which you seemed, certainly, to perceive and act upon information — information that you did not even realize you possessed.

Some of Ruburt's notes that you have not seen have further important insights as to such activity. The main point is indeed the importance of accepting (underlined) a different kind of overall orientation — one that is indeed not any secondary adjunct, but a basic part of human nature. As your own and Ruburt's notes state, Ruburt's more clearly, this involves an entirely different relationship of the self you know with time. You can make your own connections here, as per Ruburt's camera experience, and your own dreams of late.

Important misunderstandings involving time have been in a large measure responsible for many of Ruburt's difficulties, and also of your own, though they have been of a lesser nature. All of this involves relating to reality in a more natural, and therefore magical, fashion. There is certainly a kind of natural physical time in your experience, and in the experience of any creature. It involves the rhythm of the seasons — the days and nights and tides and so forth. In the light of that kind of physical time, which is involved within earthly biology, there is no (pause) basic cultural time. That is, to this natural rhythm you have culturally added the idea of clocks, moments and hours and so forth, which you have transposed over nature's rhythms.

(9:05.) Such a cultural time works well overall for the civilization that concentrates upon partialities, bits and pieces, assembly lines, promptness of appointments, and so forth. It fits an industrialized society as you understand it.

The time that any artistic creator is involved with follows earth's own time, however. The creator's time rises out of the seasons and the tides, even though in your society you make a great effort to fit the creator's time into what I will call assembly-line time. If you are a writer or an artist, then it seems that you must produce so many paintings or books or whatever as, say, an automobile worker must process so many pieces of the overall car chassis. Particularly if you want to make a living at your art, you fall into the frame of mind in which you think that "each minute is valuable" — but what you mean is that each minute must be a minute of production. But each moment must be valuable in itself, whatever you do with it.

Ruburt culturally has felt, for many reasons that have been discussed, that each moment must be devoted to work. You have to some extent felt the same. I said that the artistic creator operates in the time of the seasons and so forth, in a kind of natural time — but that natural time is far different than you suppose. Far richer, and it turns inward and outward and backward and forward upon itself.

Being your own natural and magical self when you dream, you utilize information that is outside of the time context experienced by the so-called rational mind. The creative abilities operate in the same fashion, appearing within consecutive time, but with the main work done outside of it entirely. When you

· 3 ·

finished your project,[4] you had several days of feeling miserable, but you caught yourself and turned yourself around beautifully, and you have every right to congratulate yourself in that regard.

The same thing happened to Ruburt, and to some extent, with some individual variations, the same causes were involved. When you were both working on those projects your cultural time was taken up in a way you found acceptable. Creative time and cultural time to some extent merged, in that you could see daily immediate evidence of creativity's product, coming out of the typewriters, say, like any product off an assembly line. You were "using" time as your cultural training told you to do.

Do you want a break?

("No.")

(9:25.) When the projects were done, particularly with Ruburt, there was still the cultural belief that time should be so used (underlined), that creativity must be directed and disciplined to fall into the proper time slots. In other words, to some extent or another he tried to use an assembly-line kind of time for your creative productivity. This may work when manuscripts are being typed, and so much physical labor is involved, but overall you are using the "wrong" approach to time, particularly for any creative artist. This again applies particularly to Ruburt, though you are not exonerated in that regard *(with some humor.*

(Pause.) There is much material here that I will give you, because it is important that you understand the different ways of relating to reality, and how those ways create the experienced events.

You have not really, either of you, been ready to drastically alter your orientations, but you are approaching that threshold. As Ruburt's notes also mention, the "magical approach" means that you actually change your methods of dealing with problems, achieving goals, and satisfying means. You change over to the methods of the natural person. They are indeed, then, a part of your private experience. They are not esoteric methods, but you must be convinced that they are the natural methods by which man is meant to handle his problems and approach his challenges.

I use the word "methods" because you understand it, but actually we are speaking about an approach to life, a magical or natural approach to life that is man's version of the animal's natural instinctive behavior in the universe.

That approach does indeed fly in direct contradiction to the learned methods you have been taught. You have held on to those methods to varying degrees, since after all it seems that the world shares them. They are understood ways of dealing with events. Once again, however, with the experience of the last few days, you are both astonished by the magical ease by which work — real work — can be accomplished: events perceived out of place and time and so forth.

All of that can be transferred to other areas of your lives, and in particular to Ruburt's [physical] difficulties, I do understand your joint concern, and in holding the session I know you want specific answers — which I always give to the best of my ability.

It certainly seems that the best way to get specific answers is to ask specific questions, and the rational mind thinks first of all of something like a list of questions. In that regard, Ruburt's response before such a session is natural, and to an extent magical, because he knows that no matter what he has been taught, he must to some degree (underlined) forget the questions and the mood that accompanies them with one level of his consciousness, in order to create the proper kind of atmosphere at another level of consciousness — an atmosphere that allows the answers to come even though they may be presented in a different way than that expected by the rational mind.

What we will be discussing for several sessions, with your permission jointly — and, I hope, with your joint enthusiasm — will be the magical approach to reality, and to your private lives specifically, in order to create that kind of atmosphere in which the answers become experienced (underlined).

(9:39.) Trying to fit the great thrust of creativity into assembly-line time is in itself bound to lead to conflicts, dissatisfactions, and frustrations. If the proper creative and magical orientation is kept primarily in mind, other things will fall into place. You do not say to the creative self, "Now it is 7:30. People are at their assembly lines. I am at my desk: produce."

Assembly-line time does not really value time — only as time can be used for definite prescribed purposes. In that framework, to enjoy time becomes a weakness or a vice, and both of you to some extent have so considered time. With creative people strongly gifted, as in your cases, the natural person is very prominent, no matter what you do. It therefore strongly resents any basically meaningless constraints placed about its experience. It knows, for example, how to enjoy each day, how to collect creative insights from each and every encounter, how to enrich itself physically through household chores or other activities. It dislikes being told that it must work thus and so at command of unreasonable restraints.

The natural person is anything but irrational. It gathers all of experience together and transforms it, so many of your problems have been caused by applying the wrong kind of orientation to your lives and activities.

I say wrong, meaning no moral judgment, but the application of one method to a pursuit that cannot be adequately expressed in such a fashion. The assembly-line time and the beliefs that go along with it have given you many benefits as a society, but it should not be forgotten that the entire framework was initially set up to <u>cut down</u> on impulses, creative thought, or any other activities that would lead to anything but the mindless repetition of one act after another *(intently)*.

In other words, that entire framework is meant to give you a standardized, mass-produced version of reality. None of its concepts can *(knocking the table)* rationally be applied to creative endeavors. The orientation that gives you the creative achievement lies in the opposite direction.

Creativity itself has its own built-in discipline, the kind that, for example, in a dream can rummage through the days of the future to find precisely the data required to make a specific point.

All of this material applies to Ruburt's condition, and an understanding of it will create the climate in which beneficial results can appear.

Do you want a break?

("Yes.")

Then we will continue.

(9:53–10:05.)

When Ruburt finished his project *(God of Jane)*, he found himself with all of that time that was supposed to be <u>used</u>

(underlined). He also became aware once again of his limitations, physically speaking: <u>There was not much, it seemed, he could do but work</u>, so he took the rational approach — and <u>it</u> says that to solve the problem you worry about it.

At the same time the natural person did emerge. Ruburt followed his impulses and interpreted your dreams — all of which led you both into fresh creative activity. But it was not work, you see. What he needed to do was really relax, not prove that he could or should or must immediately begin another book. <u>True creativity comes from enjoying the moments, which then fulfill themselves, and a part of the creative process is indeed the art of relaxation, the letting go, for that triggers magical activity</u>, and that is what Ruburt must learn.

I will have quite a bit to say, again, about the magical approach, and I do think the term will help each of you bring Framework 2 far more into your experience. As far as Ruburt's present situation, he should not wear, say, one pair of jeans for a week, but instead alternate, with two or three pairs that can be worn of course many times.

The underclothes are a poor kind, both for the weather and for someone whose motions are restricted. He should also vary his nightwear more. Your suggestion that he walk one more time, when he mentioned a program, was excellent. It made him realize how limited his activity had become, and again following the prescribed rational prescription, he worried about it.

Then he contrasted his present position against the idealized desired one, all of which served to lower his mood, and intensify his susceptibility to the heat, chair pressure, and so forth.

I want it understood that we are indeed dealing with two

entirely different approaches to reality and to solving problems — methods we will here call the rational method and the magical one. The rational approach works quite well in certain situations, such as mass production of goods, or in certain kinds of scientific measurements — but all in all the rational method, as it is understood and used, does not work as an overall approach to life, or in the solving of problems that involve subjective rather than objective measurements or calculations.

Those methods work least of all for any art. It is a trite statement, perhaps, but the ruler's measurements have absolutely nothing to do with the measurements made by the heart, and they can never be used to express the incalculable measurements that are made automatically by the smallest cell.

The rational mind alone, as it is presently used (because it is a rather artificial construct, a function given prominence), can never understand the dream measurements that you undertook in order to come up with the Brenner dream.[5]

(10:24.) Ruburt kept a strong rational approach to make sure that he was keeping his psychic activity in line, because in your society this seemed the only rational thing to do *(ironically).* Your problems have not been solved, then, largely of course because you have taken the wrong approach, and that is because you were jointly not convinced as yet. You still held to those trained beliefs. In that regard, Ruburt has suffered more than you have.

The old beliefs, of course, and the rational approach, are everywhere reinforced, and so it does indeed have a great weight. The magical approach has far greater weight, if you use it and allow yourselves to operate in that fashion, for it has the weight of your basic natural orientation. The rational approach is the superimposed one. I think that you are both ready to understand that.

In this session is material that will indeed allow Ruburt to get out of the present situation, but we will continue the discussion at our next session. I have given you some such material before, as I intend to give you shortly. With your own recent experiences, however, the material will be more meaningful and significant now, so that you can indeed put it this time to better use, and I will also be somewhat more specific. I will also go into any questions you want regarding your later dreams or their implications. It is good to be back with you again. End of session, and a fond and magical good evening to you both.

(*"Thank you, Seth."* 10:30 P.M.)

NOTES: SESSION OF AUGUST 6, 1980

1. Seth is the "energy personality essence" Jane speaks for while in a trance or dissociated state. Since he calls Jane by the male-oriented name of her larger or whole self, "Ruburt," it follows that Seth also calls her "he," "his," and "him."

2. It's true, following the enthusiasm we felt when Seth first described Frameworks 1 and 2 three years ago, that Jane and I haven't consistently tried all that hard to draw from that overall concept the results we think we consciously want.

In *Mass Events*, Seth speaks often about Frameworks 1 and 2. From my opening notes for Session 814, which Jane held on October 8, 1977 for that book:

"Then, in a private session held on the evening of September 17, 1977, Seth came through with a very exciting concept called 'Framework 1 and Framework 2.' Jane and I were so struck by the practical, far-reaching implications of this proposition that we began a concerted effort to put it to use in daily life. Briefly and very simply, Seth maintains that

Framework 2, or inner reality, contains the creative source from which we form all events, and that by the proper focusing of attention we can draw from that vast subjective medium everything we need for a constructive, positive life in Framework 1, or physical reality."

Seth speaks in Session 826, held for *Mass Events* on March 8, 1978:

"Any event, therefore, has an invisible <u>thickness</u>, a multidimensional basis. Your skies are filled with breezes, currents, clouds, sunlight, dust particles and so forth. The sky vaults above the entire planet. The invisible [vault of] Framework 2 contains endless patterns that change as, say, clouds do — that mix and merge to form your psychological climate. Thoughts have what we will for now term <u>electromagnetic properties</u>. In those terms your thoughts mix and match with others in Framework 2, creating mass patterns that form the overall psychological basis behind world events. Again, however, Framework 2 is not neutral, but automatically inclined toward what we will here term good or constructive developments. It is a growth medium. Constructive or 'positive' feelings or thoughts are more easily materialized than 'negative' ones because they are in keeping with Framework 2's characteristics."

3. Seth describes the camera episode after 9:15 P.M. in the next session, which Jane held on August 11.

4. I had just finished typing the manuscript for Jane/Seth's *The Individual and the Nature of Mass Events*, and Jane had just finished typing the manuscript for her own *God of Jane.* Prentice-Hall published both books.

5. See my account of the Brenner dream, Jane's interpretation of it, and Seth's material on it, in the August 11 session.

SESSION TWO

AUGUST 11, 1980
8:43 P.M., MONDAY

(T*oday I bought Jane a "water cushion" to aid in her sitting difficulties, but upon filling it after supper we didn't think it would work. I also bought her three kinds of underclothes to try . . . Before the session we spent an hour or so watching the Democratic National Convention in New York City. We saw the first session, in which the Carter forces, who wanted a "closed" convention, defeated the Kennedy forces, who wanted an "open" convention.*

(I told Jane, joking, that the Democrats might achieve a show of unity in their convention, but that come election time in November they might end up saying something like: "Well, we lost but we were united" against Reagan. To me the political situation, meaning a choice between Carter and Reagan, is almost intolerable, and I wondered why our country had chosen this time of travail, as they say.

("Well," Jane said at 8:40, "I'm about as comfortable as I can get, so I might as well begin. I feel him around. At least I feel a lot better than I have been." We've read over the last session several times, and have gone over Seth's resolutions daily. Jane has also been "walking" twice daily,

using her wheeled typing table as a support — though we skipped this
evening's sojourn in lieu of TV watching. The night was humid but not
too warm. Through the open doors and windows we heard the great
rhythms of the crickets and cicadas. Then:)

Now —

("Good evening, Seth.")

Good evening. It is not that you overuse the intellect as a culture, but that you rely upon it to the exclusion of <u>all</u> other faculties in your approach to life. Period.

The intellect is brilliant, <u>but on its own, now</u> (underlined), it is indeed in its way isolated both in time and in space in a way that other portions of the personality are not. When it is <u>overly</u> stressed, with all of the usual frameworks or rationales that go along with it, it can indeed become frightened, paranoid, because it cannot really perceive events until they have already occurred. It does not know what will happen tomorrow, and since it is overly stressed, its paranoid tendencies can only fear the worst.

Now those tendencies are not natural to the intellect, but only appear when it is forced to operate in such an isolated fashion — isolated not only in time and space, but psychologically isolated from other portions of the personality that are meant to bring it additional information that it does not possess, and a kind of magical support.

The so-called rational approach to life, as it is practiced, is a highly pessimistic one, carrying along with it its own methods and "solutions" to problems, its own means of achieving ends and satisfying desires. Many people are so steeped in that approach to life that they become psychologically blind to any other kind of orientation. Such is obviously not the case with you and Ruburt, or you would not be having this session, or any other such activity.

The rational approach of course suits certain kinds of people better than others, even while it still carries its disadvantages. You have been living in an industrialized, scientific society, so that the benefits and the great disadvantages of the rational approach appear everywhere in the social and political world. Artists of any kind find such an approach the least friendly, for it directly contradicts the vast thrust of man's creativity in several important areas. You, however, and Ruburt, do have evidence that hardbed reality is quite different. In the past you have both felt at some disadvantage yourselves, feeling our work to be theoretically fascinating, creatively valid, but not necessarily containing any statement about any kind of "scientifically valid" hardbed reality. *(All with much emphasis.*

(8:56.) You did not think you were dealing with fiction. On the other hand, you were not willing to call it fact, either. You are, in fact, dealing with a larger version of fact from which — as I have said before — the world of fact emerges.

There have been numerous fascinating bits of evidence in your own lives, apart from these sessions, though certainly to some extent stimulated by the knowledge you gain in the sessions. They remain isolated bits, odds and ends, in which case they begin to present you with a larger factual representation of reality.

All of this material applies to your lives in general and to Ruburt's physical condition, because you must be clear in your minds as to your own status in that regard, and much of this material will clear the air and dissolve lingering doubts; doubts that cause both of you — but Ruburt in particular — to hold on to the rational approach in a misguided effort to maintain what he thinks of as a balanced viewpoint and open mind. It seems, because of the definitions you have been taught, that there is only one narrow kind of rationality, and that if you forsake the boundary of that narrow definition, then you become irrational, fanatic, mad, or whatever (*all very emphatically*).

The thin, cold "rationality" that is recognized as such is instead a fake veneer covering a far deeper spontaneous rationality, and it is the existence of that magical rationality that provides the basis for the intellect to begin with. The rationality that you accept is then but one small clue as to the spontaneous inner rationality that is a part of each natural person.

Now: In one dream when you were asleep, when you were seemingly not rational, when your intellect was seemingly not operating, you perceived information about your past physical environment. You saw your old neighborhood (*on June 10, 1980*)[1] — the Brenner's place, with animal and industrial waste all over the yard. Symbolically you saw the situation in your own fashion, but you knew that the Brenner's property had been polluted. You still have a love of that area. You are in a certain correspondence with it. In a fashion, you keep your eye out for information regarding it.

You are also somewhat idealizing the past, however, so you did not simply get the information "straight on," but you received it in such a fashion that it made its own psychological points also, and was furthermore wound into other action not only within that dream, but in a series of dreams.

(*9:15.*) The dream made its point, whether or not you read the article that later appeared (*in the Elmira paper*). The dream made its point, in fact, whether or not you remembered it, though you did. You remembered it because you wanted to bring into your conscious range instances of your own greater knowing. The portion of you that formed the dream knew of the pollution; but also knew of the award, the newspaper article, and of your habit of reading

· 15 ·

the evening's paper. All of that involves a psychological motion of natural, magical import. It shows you that the rules of the rational world are filled with holes. It shows you that the rational world's views do not represent the bulwarks of safety, but are instead barriers to the full use of the intellect, and of the intuitions.

Ruburt, having interpreted your dream, looked wide-awake but relaxed through his studio into the kitchen. He thought of asking you to take a snapshot of the table with your camera, showing the partially-opened front door, so that later he could paint the scene. Your camera could not take in all of that, a fact he never thought of. Less than two minutes later, you came out into his studio with the camera that you had not used for months. Ruburt had also been thinking newly about the magical approach from ideas in your own notes[2] that he had just read. You came out as if in answer. As if to say, "Yes, the magical approach does indeed operate, and this is how."

Ruburt's state of mind was in correspondence with your own state of mind, even as you are in some kind of correspondence with your old environment, so in these cases you have a free flow of information at other levels.

Now when you understand that intellectually, then the intellect can take it for granted that its own information is not all the information you possess. It can realize that its own knowledge represents the tip of the iceberg. As you apply that realization to your life you begin to realize furthermore that in practical terms you are indeed supported by a greater body of knowledge than you consciously realize, and by the magical, spontaneous fountain of action that forms your existence. The intellect can then realize that it does not have to go it all alone: Everything does not have to be reasoned out, even to be understood.

(Jane delivered the above paragraph of material as Seth with much emphasis and conviction, as she has for much of this session. I think it excellent, and plan to make copies to pin on my studio wall for easy reference.)

This information is factual. I am not saying that I do not use analogies often, or that I am not forced at times into symbolic statements, but when I am I always say so, and even those statements are my best representations of facts too large for your definitions. The intellect, then, <u>can</u> and does form strong paranoid tendencies when it is put in the position of believing that it must solve all personal problems alone — or nearly — and certainly when it is presented with any picture of worldwide predicaments.

The rational approach, built up around this framework, insists that the best way to solve a problem is to concentrate upon it, to project its effects into the future, to ruminate upon its consequences, "to stare at the bare facts head on."

This brings about an atmosphere in which the problem is compounded. The intellect on its own — so it seems — must deal not only with the problem today, but with its effects in the projected disastrous tomorrows. This well-intentioned concentration, this determination to solve the problem, this rational approach, then causes an even deeper sense of inadequacy. The concentration upon the problem brings about a kind of mechanical repetition, a repeated type of hypnotic focus.

(9:36.) The intellect is a great organizer — along certain lines, now — so if this concentration is continued it begins to organize its perceptions and experience along the same lines. It is a kind of misguided attempt to find order by finding data that agrees with itself. It collects evidence, then, to prove its point, because the rational mind, as you understand it, must have an acceptable reason for <u>everything</u> (underlined) *(all intently).*

In the meantime, of course, quite valid rockbed evidence that does not fit into the picture gradually becomes discarded, ignored, thrown away. It is there but it is not used. It disappears as evidence, becomes inactive. That method of problem-solving, need I say, is a poor one, and if anything it causes far more problems than it ever solves.

In terms of Ruburt's condition, he often thinks that he is "faced with the evidence" that his condition is not improving, that it is growing worse, that all the evidence says such conditions do deteriorate rather than improve. He sometimes thinks that he is being realistic with such thoughts.

What happens, of course, is the process I have just outlined. Other quite real, quite physical evidence — always, now, apparent in his body at any given time — is ignored as nonessential, too trivial to bother with, or take seriously, because it does not fit into the so-called rational picture that has been developed.

(*"Do you want to give an example?" I asked Seth, but Jane went on speaking so smoothly that I wondered if he/she had heard the question.*)

The process is exactly as given in the paragraph above, so I want that understood. Any improvement, unless stated, is almost overlooked, not considered as much hard evidence, while any difficulties definitely are considered hard evidence because they fit into the overall data-collecting intellect, as stated above. They are significant, while the improvements do not seem to be nearly as much so.

(*Now Seth began to give information relative to my question.*)

Ruburt has had some release in the past week of the jaw, neck, and shoulder areas. His eyes at times, on three or four occasions, read remarkably better. For some time his ankles and knees have had greater freedom of motion — in certain motions — but all such evidence is ignored, largely — or worse, it is viewed ironically, since he is not walking any better.

You picked up the information about the Brenners because you were in correspondence with that environment. You picked up inner evidence in that regard. You ignored countless other bits of information. Ruburt picked up your own camera activities because he was in correspondence with you. He must be in correspondence with the evidence of mobility that his body tries to give him, so that it can build up a new picture of his body.

You change your focus point. You change what you consider significant. This session brings us to the beginning of a discussion of the magical approach to life, to the solving of problems. I hope to stress what to do, rather than what not to do, although at times I must make the distinction clear.

If you understand this session thoroughly, and if you have the intent to really change your orientation, then the atmosphere will automatically be created in which desired changes occur.

End of session —

("Thank you.")

— and a fond good evening.

(9:56 P.M. As soon as she was out of trance I told Jane the session was an excellent one. I was also quite irritated, because Seth's information had the ability to make things seem self-evident; from that point one was always left wondering how anything so basically clear and simple could be so easily missed and/or misinterpreted by those who most dearly wanted to put it to use. I've experienced these phenomena often in personal sessions, and each time end up resolving to do better next time — to see more clearly, to do all of those things that will easily and effortlessly bring the desired results. Jane often feels the same way, though I don't think she has so much lately, judging from certain remarks she's made. Yet this kind of

material gives one hope, and considering it can lead to at least momentary feelings of true understanding and concomitant hope, on my part, at least. The thing is, I really believe the information is good, and that it can work, that basically it's the best kind of information people can get.

(I suppose my own irritation because of the points listed above communicated itself to Jane easily enough. We had a lively and beneficial discussion because of our feelings, though, so all in all the session is a very good one.[3] I want to arrange my approach to Seth's latest book, Dreams, "Evolution," and Value Fulfillment, *so that I can quote part of this session in a note.)*

Notes: Session of August 11, 1980

1. From my dream notebook: "Dream, very early Tuesday morning, June 10, 1980.

"In vivid color: I lived in my parents' house at 704 North Wilbur Avenue, in Sayre, Pennsylvania. I was my present age, 61. That the house had long been sold, that my parents had died in the early 1970s, and that Jane and I had been married for 26 years and lived in Elmira, New York, were irrelevant in the dream. Jane and my parents were not in it, nor were any members of the Brenner family.

"Years ago, after my brothers and I had left 704 to follow our own life paths, the Brenner family had built a house next door to our parents' place. This represents a contradiction in the dream — or, rather, that I tried to combine two spans of time. On a summer evening after dusk in the dream, I went for a walk with Floyd Waterman (I'll call him), a 'real' friend from Elmira who was visiting me. Floyd is a contractor.

"To reach Wilbur Avenue we cut across the tennis court, of grass, that my father had built for his teen-age sons so long ago. In physical life the Brenner house sits where the court had existed. Just beyond the court, and next to the sidewalk, grew an old shagbark hickory tree that I had always loved, and still remember vividly. The tree would be in the Brenner's front yard now.

"As Floyd and I cut across the court I saw that the Brenner's lawn was despoiled with a mixture of animal and industrial waste, like pollution. 'What's that?' I exclaimed to Floyd, as I saw a large dark shape near the hickory tree. At first shock I thought it was a deer that might have been killed by a car the night before, say. It lay on its side with its back to us. Then to my amazement I saw that the supposed animal was actually the broken remnants of a hollow, life-sized metal statue of a deer that had stood for years in the front yard of a house on Harrison Street, in Sayre, at the other end of town. The house had been owned by the Maynards, who had no children. When my next-youngest brother and I were in grade school, our family had lived a few houses down Harrison from the Maynards. Mr. Maynard had been a carpenter. He and his wife and my parents had been friends. All of us kids in the neighborhood had been fascinated by the deer, which had been painted brown. We had climbed all over it. My father had photographed it.

"Now I saw, again to my surprise, that the deer had been broken in pieces and lay in the Brenner's front yard, where the hickory tree had stood a moment ago. I exclaimed to Floyd Waterman that vandals had done the damage — young kids that I knew were causing trouble in the neighborhood. They'd broken off the animal's legs. The Brenner's front door was open and I saw the warm yellow light in their living room. I knew that I had to run into their house and tell them about the poor broken deer lying in their front yard."

On July 23, 1980 — 13 days after I had my dream — the writer of a story in the Elmira *Star-Gazette* described how the Brenner family won an out-of-court settlement of over $10,000 from the Borough of Sayre and a large store owned by a well-known supermarket chain. The store is located a couple of blocks from the Brenner home, and just off North Wilbur Avenue. Construction at the store had overloaded sewage pipes and caused them to back up after rain storms, filling the basement of the Brenner house with sewage several times.

I hadn't consciously known about the situation in any way. Indeed, I haven't been to Sayre in many months, even though my old home town is only 18 miles away. Jane hasn't been in our car for some time now, and I leave her alone in the house as little as possible.

❋   ❋   ❋

Here is Jane's interpretation of my dream:

"Rob's dream states quite clearly, precognitively, about the pollution of the Brenner property from the supermarket just up the street. Many of Rob's dreams have involved a nostalgic view of the past, plus questions of safety and danger. I think he picked up on the precognitive element to show himself that his pictures of the past were too idealistic.

"The statue of the deer represents that idealistic image of the past; finding it broken in Brenner's yard connects its real environment where Rob lived as a small boy [on Harrison Street] to Wilbur Avenue where he lived later; meaning that he'd idealized both backgrounds. The statue of the deer, an inanimate animal, contrasts with the waste left by a living animal. Idealized ones, statues, don't leave waste, but they don't live either.

"Floyd Waterman represents someone who has a connection with living animals in the present [on his farm], and connects the times in the dream, since he also is in the construction business and does carpentry work —and the man who owned the deer was a carpenter. Rob's also had other dreams involving Floyd and animals. . . ."

2.   Seth refers to a portion of the notes I wrote on the afternoon of August 5, 1980 — the day before Jane held her first session on *The Magical Approach:*

"It was hard to reduce my insight to words, but when I described it to Jane at our lunch table, she said it made sense to her. The insight was triggered by a remark she made while we were eating, as she read one of the letters I'd just picked up at the mailbox.

"The letter-writer described several well-known esoteric organizations that he belonged to — while also asking for personal help from Jane. 'He wants magic,' Jane said. Her comment reminded me of some material I'd written last month, and had mentioned to her a few times since — that over very long spans of time the earth and all of its creatures stay the same, relatively speaking, and that only human beings, with their ideas of 'progress' and 'development' change.

"The insight that flashed into my consciousness was that human beings haven't changed either, really, that our more complicated mental processes only make it seem that we have. Coupled with this is the idea that magic, as we call it, reflects a basic part of our natural mental equipment and abilities, but that our present course of action, our focusing upon the material and the intellectual — the 'reasonable' portions of our psyche — has created artificial divisions, in which magic seems quite 'unreasonable' or unreal. Actually, our need for magic is a very real, vital, and integral portion of our psyches.

"The conscious idea of magic, then, is a mask, or contrived version, of the psyche's innate clairvoyant, telepathic, and precognitive abilities. We permit distorted versions of those attributes to surface as magic, as entertainment — which thus relieves us of the need to take them seriously. That's the course our species has chosen during much of our recorded history, so far, and for many reasons.

"I think that I brought my magical insight into consciousness also because of some of my recent dreams, that seem to contain precognitive and/or clairvoyant elements. The Brenner dream is one of those. Jane has been doing invaluable work for me recently, interpreting those dreams. Indeed, she's the one who's dug up many of the dream and real-life connections.

"Added a little later: Jane said this material on the magical personality '. . . really turned me on.' She's been doing some writing of her own on our magical orientation. I told her that her material could easily go into a chapter of one of her books."

3. And yes, the situation can be reversed, too: Seth can get irritated/frustrated with Jane and me. This excerpt is from the private session of November 11, 1979: ". . . the same kind of reactions, however, are involved in all activities, and it is sometimes frustrating for me that you cannot perceive the fascinating facets of any event. You still — and I do not simply mean you two alone — do not feel the unsurpassable force

that thoughts have. You do not understand that they do form events, that to change events you must first change thoughts. You get what you concentrate upon."

See Appendix B for Jane's material, written later, which she intended to go with this Session Two.

SESSION THREE

MAN AND OTHER SPECIES. MISTAKES AS CORRECTIVE ACTION.
DEFINITION OF THE MAGICAL APPROACH.

AUGUST 13, 1980
8:57 P.M., WEDNESDAY

(I *finished typing the last half of Monday's session just before the session
tonight. I reminded Jane that I think it's an excellent one, and that I
want to type copies for us of the material between 9:15 and 9:36, wherein
Seth explains that the intellect needs to realize that it doesn't have to go it
alone, that it is supported and aided by other portions of the self. I think
this insight can help Jane greatly. I also told her I want to quote portions
of Monday's session in Seth's current book,* Dreams.

*(A note: The Democratic National Convention is in its third day. As I
typed away after supper, I could tell that Jane was listening to the speeches
on TV in the living room. Then I realized I'd goofed: Last Saturday, our
local paper had carried a short article to the effect that a psychic we'd
heard of had predicted recently that Senator Robert Byrd of West Virginia
would obtain the Democratic nomination for president, after a deadlock
between Carter and Kennedy developed at the convention. I read the article and called it to Jane's attention. I'd meant to save it, but instead the
paper ended up bundled up with the trash for pickup this morning. Since
the Carter forces won the fight to keep the convention "closed" during its*

first, Monday session, this assures Carter the nomination on the first ballot. Thus the psychic is wrong in the prediction, which evidently obtained national circulation.

(At least, I told Jane tonight after I'd remembered that I'd forgotten to clip the article for my predictions file, we know where the article is on file, where it can be located if necessary: at the newspaper office. I speculated about the reactions of public personalities when their predictions don't work out. I hoped their errors are not rationalized, or made just for the publicity, since the psychics have to live with them. We'll keep a lookout for any follow-up articles on the subject, but I suppose it will die like any other item in yesterday's news. What do the predictors secretly think in such situations, though? No one is perfect. Jane hasn't tried to predict similar events. For some of Jane's predictions see Appendix A.

(Jane, for her part, said she didn't particularly feel like having a session tonight, that she was "doing it just to do it." I suggested that by all means she have it. She's been feeling better at times, so our new program is getting some kind of results.)

Good evening.

("Good evening, Seth.")

(With some dry amusement:) Now: I myself have heard it said that all other species preserve nature, while man has a propensity for destroying it.

(See my notes of July 17, 1980.[1] Seth continued to stare at me as he proceeded in the same manner:)

I have myself heard it said that other creatures behave with a natural grace, save man. I have myself heard it said that all of nature is *(pause)* content unto itself save man, who is filled with discontent. Such thoughts follow "naturally" the dictums of so-called rational thought. When you think such thoughts, you think of them at the most strained level of intellectual speculation — that is, the thoughts seem self-evident to the intellect that is forced to operate by itself, relatively speaking, divorced from the self's other faculties. It then does indeed seem that man is somehow apart from nature — or worse, an ungrateful blight, almost a parasite, upon the face of the planet.

That view itself is a symptom of the intellect's difficulty. In the position in which your culture places the intellect, it does (underlined) see itself quite alone, separated both from other portions of the personality, from other creatures, and from nature itself. Therefore science, for example, says that creatures — except for man — operate by blind instinct, and that term is meant to explain all of the complicated behavior of the other species. Therefore the gulf between man and animals, the intellect and nature, seems to deepen.

In those terms (underlined), it is quite as truthful to say — as I have said before — that man's intellect is also instinctive. He begins thinking at once. He cannot help but use his intellect. The intellect, again, operates magically, spontaneously, automatically. Its most keen reasoning processes rise as a result of that natural magical action (deliberately).

(Pause.) The intellect has been taught to divorce itself from its source. It realizes in that regard a sense of powerlessness, for to some extent it is philosophically cut off from its own source of power. When it looks, therefore, at the world of political events, the problems seem insoluble. Man makes many decisions that may seem quite wrong to the intellect because of its belief systems, and because it is so cut off from other sources of information. A goodly number of those mistaken decisions, or "poor moves," often represent self-corrective actions, decisions taken on knowledge not consciously perceived, but this escapes your consciousness.

(9:14.) In the same way, some private-life decisions or events may appear disadvantageous to the intellect for the same reasons, while instead they are also self-corrective measures that you are not able to perceive <u>because</u> of your beliefs. The rational approach, as it is now used, carries a basic assumption that anything that is wrong will get worse. That belief of course is highly detrimental because it runs <u>against</u> the basic principles of life. Were this the case in your terms of history, the world would never have lasted a century. It is interesting to note that even before medical science, there were a goodly number of healthy populations. No disease rubbed out the entire species.

When you believe that the worst will happen you must always be on guard. In your culture people use the term "intellect" almost like a weapon to protect themselves against impending disaster. They must be alert for dangers of all kinds. They begin to collect evidence of danger so that any other kind of orientation to life seems foolhardy, and to be a realist means in that framework to look out for the worst.

First of all, if you realize that the intellect itself is <u>a part of</u> nature, a part of the natural person, a part of magical processes, then you need not overstrain it, force it to feel isolated, or put it in a position in which paranoid tendencies develop. It is itself supported, as your intuitions are, by life's magical processes. It is supported by the greater energy that gave you and the world birth. That power is working in the world, and in the world of politics, as it is in the world of nature, since you make that distinction.

When you follow that so-called rational approach, however, you are bound to feel threatened, divorced from your body. Your thoughts and your body seem separate. Divisions seem to appear between the mental and the physical, where again each are supported by those magical processes. That rational approach goes against what I can only call life's directives and life's natural rhythms. It is contradictory to biological integrity, and again, it does not make sense.

That rational approach is, of course, connected now with scientific ideas mentioned earlier: life surrounded by chaos, the struggle for survival, and so forth. I do not mean to put down the intellect. It is highly important, but it is, if you will forgive me, as natural as a cat's whiskers. It is not some adjunct to nature, but a part of it.

(Seth may have made his humorous reference to a cat's whiskers when he did because our cat, Billy, had just meowed rather frantically as he chased a dusty-looking moth through the living room.)

The magical approach takes it for granted, in the simplest terms, that the life of any individual will fulfill itself, will develop and mature, that the environment and the individual are uniquely suited and work together. This sounds very simple. In verbal terms, however, those are the beliefs (if you will) of each c-e-l-l *(spelled)*. They are imprinted in each chromosome, in each atom. They provide a built-in faith that pervades each living creature, each snail, each hair on your head. Those ingrained beliefs are, of course, biologically pertinent, providing the impetus of all growth and development.

(9:32.) Each cell *(pause)* believes in a better tomorrow *(quietly, with amusement)*. I am, I admit, personifying our cell here, but the statement has a firm truth. Furthermore, each cell contains within itself a belief and an understanding of its own inevitability. It knows it lives beyond its death, in other words.

The idea of heaven, for all of its distortions, has operated as a theoretical framework, assuring the intellect of its survival. Science has believed to the contrary in the utter annihilation of the intellect after death, and since man had by then placed all of his identification with the intellect, this was a shattering blow to it. It denied man a necessary biological imperative *(all intently)*.

All of these reasons lie beneath man's mass problems, and apply in each life. I want to note, again, that Ruburt earlier decided to bank on his intellect as a child, rather than upon beauty, as he felt his mother had. In his case also, as given in the past, he felt that the feminine qualities were those opposed to intellectual development. *(Pause.)* He was gifted intuitively <u>and</u> intellectually, however, and naturally was propelled toward growth in both areas — areas that he felt stressed contradictory rather than complementary characteristics.[2]

Now take any other person — or rather, more to the point, any other <u>woman</u> — in the so-called psychic field. Ruburt tries to prove that he is reasonable, <u>rational</u> (underlined), where such people, he feels, have never learned to use their powers of reason, and instead trust every stray thought that comes into their heads. So to doubt himself was protective.

(Long pause.) He also felt that the questioning power of the intellect was not just <u>one</u> of its functions — which it is — but its primary purpose, which it is not. In your terms the intellect's primary function is to make clear deductions and distinctions involving the personality's relationship with the world. Your society, however, has indeed considered the rational approach to be the masculine-favored one — so Ruburt had an additional reason in that regard to be such a proponent of the rational approach. All of the beliefs connected with the sex were of course erroneous, but they were part and parcel of that "rational" framework itself.

(9:44.) It is certainly too simple to say what I am going to say,

yet it is almost as if you would be better off turning the entire rational approach upside down, taking it for granted that all of its assumptions were false, for they are indeed more false than true *(intently)*. Again, you see, the divisions are arbitrary on your part. The intellect is, again, the result of highly spontaneous processes of which it itself knows nothing, and the intuitions that are considered so undisciplined and unreasonable are based upon calculations far more spectacular than those of which the conscious mind can conceive. The intellect could not follow them, so the distinctions are not basic: They are the result of beliefs and habitual usage. Therefore, of course, I speak of them separately, as you think of them.

The magical approach takes it for granted that the human being is a united creature, fulfilling purposes in nature even as the animals do, whether or not those purposes are understood. *(Pause.)* The magical approach takes it for granted that each individual has a future, a fulfilling one, even though death may be tomorrow. The magical approach takes it for granted that the means for development are within each individual, and that fulfillment will happen naturally. Overall, that approach operates in your world. If it did not, there would be no world. If the worst was bound to happen, as the scientists certainly think, even evolution, in their terms, would have been impossible, of course — a nice point to put somewhere *(all intently)*.

You needed this background, for I want to build up the atmosphere in which this magical approach can be comprehended. Then specific material can be utilized.

In your dream[3] you were, of course, in the process of forming new ideas about the nature of the magical self *(through my art)* and also in your way working that idea out through imagery. The dream is above all an example of "work" being done at other levels of awareness.

Ruburt's [recent] mental conversation with "Mary,"[4] and your own dream about Mary with the sketchbook sheets[5] — all of these experiences are indications of the exquisite kind of reasoning that goes on at the levels of awareness that are usually considered unreasonable. That kind of material enriches the intellect and reassures it.

One note: Do have Ruburt tell you how he is doing moodwise, for now you can help him there. He must realize that relaxation is also a part of the creative process. Left alone, he would do "the right thing." We will continue this discussion at our next session, and in the meantime be on the lookout for other hints and clues that will bring you a better idea of the magical approach.

End of session.

("Very good. Thank you.")

I wish you a magically content evening. My heartiest regards to you both.

("Thank you. The same to you."

(10:05 P.M. "I can't remember any of that," Jane said. "I just know I didn't have any of that in my head before the session."

(This is certainly magical — Jane's performance as Seth, in the sessions. This note, which I wrote a couple of days later, was inspired by Seth's material in this session:

("Seth, of course, not only dictates his magical material — the session — but must keep the whole session in mind while doing so, so that each sentence as he delivers it makes sense compared to its predecessors, and those to follow. Quite a feat on his part, and Jane's, once you stop to think about it. How is this possible? Seth has no script to go by, nor can he refer during the session to my own notes to check up on what he's already said.

("I'd say that a great memory must be involved here, coupled on deeper levels with a shortening of time as we think of it. Seth's abilities remind me of material I've written recently on how certain portions of the personality or psyche must very shrewdly and carefully construct dreams in advance, so that when the dreams are played back they render just the right message to the parts of the psyche that need it. I'm not being contradictory here when I write that the dream is a spontaneous production, also.

("These comments about Seth's abilities seem obvious when they're considered as I've just described them, yet I don't think I've thought of what Seth can do in just that way before. They make his performances all the more remarkable. See the material after 9:44 in the session of August 13, about the intellect and the 'undisciplined and unreasonable' intuitions. Actually, that whole session applies here.")

NOTES: SESSION OF AUGUST 13, 1980

1. When I wrote these notes on July 17, I hardly expected that several weeks later Seth would so effectively "put them in their place," so to speak, as he enlarged upon his discussion of the magical approach:

"'Have you ever noticed,' I said to Jane the other day, 'that everything on earth remains the same except human activity?' Jane has heard it all before. It's one of my favorite notions, and one from which I draw — with my own kind of perverse humor, it seems — great comfort and stability.

"I could list hundreds of examples of what I mean. This is one of those obvious ideas that seem childish once it's thought of. I don't care whether or not it's a profound thought; it has meaning for me. But as far as I know, we humans are the only species that's obsessed with 'change', and 'progress', and 'controlling or mastering nature'; with learning about our past and with charting our future. We strive toward an impossible, or at least rosy, future in which we will have met all of our challenges, so that we'll live in some sort of unreal wonderland on earth. What do we do next — or will we give up on that idea too? Perhaps we'll spend all of our time contemplating each other!

"Anyhow, each morning when I scatter birdfeed in the driveway of the hill house, the cardinals and the mourning doves, the chickadees and the blue jays and the other birds are waiting in the nearby Russian elms, the oak tree, or lined up on the telephone wires. Their behavior is the same each morning. If Jane and I and our house evaporated between one day and the next, and our lot was magically transformed into its native habitat, the birds would simply switch to 'natural' seeds instead of consuming the sunflower seeds, millet and other grain products that our marketplace so conveniently packages for them.

"Would those feathered species remember us? Why impose our concerns and habits upon them?

"The rabbits in our neighborhood would continue to live as usual without our help, although they might miss nibbling upon the leafy vegetables in the local gardens. The fish and all of the complex minutiae of the local river bottoms would go on living as they always have. The deer I see in the woods north of the hill house would continue to bound through the brush and among the trees. They'd live the same as ever, since it's illegal for us to feed them — although they do like to move down the hillside at night and sample certain shrubs we have kindly planted about our houses.

"In my darker moods I find myself thinking that I love the earth and everything upon it except the increasingly destructive activities of human beings — and sometimes I wonder about the human beings themselves! I love the deserts and forests, the oceans and rivers and lakes of the earth, the plains and the poles, the marshes and the mountains. And I know that in the Puerto Rico trench in the Atlantic Ocean, life in the sea at more than 8,000 feet down goes on just as it has for many millennia. It's been like that for all of the sea creatures and the flora of the oceans. It's been like that for all of the interwoven life forms of the poles and the tropics, of the deserts and woodlands and prairies. Each species lives within its environment, whatever its conditions. And I think that in its way each life form must know that and love its home, and has no desire to change or destroy it.

"So what about acid rain, say, to name but one human creation that's having a strong effect upon the earth's surface and aerial environments? We're told that it's now evident in a number of places on earth — often downwind from certain kinds of industrial activity. As to be expected, industry owners and operators maintain that their plants have little or nothing to do with the creation of the dead lakes in the Adirondacks in New York State, for example, or in certain Canadian provinces across the Great Lakes.

"Were there acid rains and dead lakes in Europe in the 1700s, for instance? There may have been, for all I know. . . ."

"Boy, Seth," I thought after tonight's session, "did I go overboard in that piece! You helped me understand some things, yet what I wrote still contains truth for me, too. I'm angry because I think — I know — that we human beings have the blessed creative capacity to do so much better. So why don't we?"

2. This session was held on August 13. Thirteen days later, Jane and I were most intrigued to read an article in a national publication in which researchers show, after eight years of tests, that not only do women do most things as well as men — they actually outperform men in many areas, both intellectually and intuitively.

For example, women test as equal to men in sensitivity to sound; clear, logical, and rational thinking; accurate reading and writing; memory for design in areas like drafting and illustration; number memory; tweezer dexterity; foresight, as in the flow of ideas; subjective personality links to specialized work.

Women exceed men in such areas as finger dexterity; accounting aptitudes; rate of idea flow, as in sales, writing, and teaching; observing small changes in physical detail; non-tangible ideas requiring complex vocabulary, as in medicine and law; the ability to visualize three-dimensional relationships, as in engineering.

According to these tests, us poor guys exceed women in only two categories: structural visualization, as in engineering, mechanics and building; and measures of simple muscular strength.

3. From my dream notebook: "Dream, very early Wednesday morning, August 13, 1980. (See my painting at the end of this session.)

"In vivid color, as usual: I dreamed that in New York City I had gone back to my first love, drawing comics. Not comic books, however, but a syndicated fantasy-adventure story to be run in color and take up a full Sunday newspaper page. Very unusual. I saw my art for the first page, perhaps half again as large as the printed version would be, lying on a flat drawing table. It was in black 'line', but also with flat washes of color. For comic books, I had drawn only the black plate. The printer had furnished the color plates.

"I was not conscious of my age, 61, in the dream, nor do I remember anything about being committed to draw a daily strip also. I had a much younger assistant who reminded me of Tom Lantini, an artist friend who had been a year behind me in Sayre High, our hometown school in Sayre, Pennsylvania. In the dream, I'd left certain areas blank in the panels making up the Sunday page, and my nameless assistant had done the art to fill in those places. My main character, a male who wore a tight-fitting Superman-type costume with a flowing cape, occupied a space several panels high right in the middle of the page — quite a daring concept for a comic layout. I knew the character type well because in the early 1940s, in 'real' life, I'd been one of the artists who had drawn the very popular comic-book hero, Captain Marvel. My dream character stood confidently facing the reader — except that I'd omitted drawing his head! My assistant had drawn the head, though, on a small separate piece of board, and protected it with a piece of tracing paper. I thought the head was too small, but well done, quite youthful with curly black hair and handsome features, as one would expect such a magical character to have. I also saw that the head was almost too youthful for the strong physique of the character I'd drawn, although I wasn't critical of this. All that remained was for the printer to fit the head and the body together. I sat at the drawing table examining the assistant's work."

My art teacher in high school, Miss Bowman, had taught Tom Lantini also — and as she had loaned me money to go to commercial art school in New York City, so had she given Tom financial aid so that he could attend the same school. See my note concerning Miss Bowman at the end of the session of September 10.

Tom started school a year after I had, and I helped him obtain a room in the same school-approved boarding house that I lived in, with other students. I told Jane that at first I was somewhat jealous of Tom, probably feeling that in some way he was intruding into my own special relationship with Miss Bowman. Jane said that makes my dream even better. This is her interpretation of the dream:

"Wed. Aug. 13 dream, 1980.

"Another great dream of Rob's. In our sessions lately Seth has been talking about the natural self or natural person, saying that it is also the magical person. In this dream Rob is in the process of working out that idea, visually. His closest connection to magic would be his comics experience when he drew Captain Marvel — a magical character. The resulting image, in two parts, shows that the idea is almost completed in his mind, just needing to be put together. In the dream he sees himself returning to the comics, only the Sunday edition (special), and the superhero character is much more prominent than the comics would ordinarily have it; the smaller head representing, I think, the idea that the intellect's place is smaller or of a lesser nature than he earlier supposed. At dream's end Rob says that the head was almost too youthful for the body he'd drawn — maybe a reminder that the natural person is younger in ways than the intellectual self. I think that Rob is himself in the dream, represented by the super character as the magical self; and also that he is the assistant who had prepared the figure's head.

"In the dream the assistant is a fellow student. I'm not sure of the connection unless it means that at the time he knew Tom, as youthful artists both Rob and Tom believed in the magical aspects of life — which now come to Rob's aid, assisting him by drawing the character's head."

4. Two days after delivering the first session for *The Magical Approach,* Jane made notes about her mental exchange with our dear longtime friend, "Mary" (the name I've given her):

"August 8, 1980.

". . . later in the night, last night, I became aware of a mental conversation between Mary and myself. She was saying that she wanted to visit, and then said she wanted to stay overnight. I became somewhat alarmed and the conversation bled off. The feeling I had was that something had happened between Mary and her new husband, an argument. She wanted to stay here for the night, perhaps leaving her son with her husband — which I didn't think was a good idea. I've picked up on Mary's relationships before. . . .

"This morning, Mary called. She sounded very down; Rob, who also talked to her, agreed. But I didn't mention my experience, much as I wanted to check it out; I didn't want to intrude. . . ."

5. My Mary dream:
"Dream, very early Sunday morning, August 10, 1980.

"Difficult to recall, and what I do recall makes no sense to me at all. In vivid color: I dreamed that Jane and I were eating at a little table in an open-air restaurant or cafe-type setting. It was a beautiful summer day. Our friend Mary came up to us. She was by herself and I don't recall her saying anything to us. She was carrying a large sketch pad, perhaps a 22-by-30-inch size. One would expect the pages of the pad to be white, ready for drawing. Instead, as Mary lifted the cover of the pad, holding the pad out for Jane and me to see, we saw that the top page was covered by a lovely large floral pattern of leaves and flowers, as one might see on bedsheets these days. I examined several pages of Mary's pad and saw that all of them were covered by the same design, in reds and greens, etc. The pattern made the pages of the pad quite useless for their ordinary purpose. I woke up several times with this dream in mind, telling myself to remember it."

And Jane's interpretation, written on the same day I had the dream:
"A terrific little dream that beautifully states its message: Mary's ideas of romance and making love (represented by modern-day flowered sheets) are being transposed from the bedroom into the area of her art, and in a way that mars the art itself. The transposition of the flowered designs of bedsheets to sheets of paper is great; Rob chose a

sketch pad rather than, say, typing paper, I think, because painting is his art while Mary's is writing. Also perhaps to make connections with Mary's sketches of her own life. Maybe by using his own art symbol, the sketch pad instead of the typing paper, Rob reinforced the idea of Mary's conflicts about the nature of her own work.

"Mary shows us the large sketch papers in an open-air restaurant — a setting where physical needs are satisfied in public. The open air specifies this public aspect, meaning that Mary's ideas are connected with social values wanting her needs satisfied in a socially acceptable public fashion. This would refer to her recent marriage. . . .

"As you can see, the dream states all this far more simply and concisely than I'm able to!"

But, I told Jane, she did a far better conscious and intuitive job of interpreting my dream of Mary than I ever could. I'm grateful!

A note: Several hours before she held today's session, Jane wrote:

"Wednesday, August 13, 1980.

"Called Mary. Since I talked to her last, she's decided to leave her husband. . . ."

Robert F. Butts (1919–): *Imaginary Character.* 1968. Oil on panel, 10 x 9⅜ in.

The individual I painted in 1968 is very similar to the magical "Captain Marvel" kind of character I created 12 years later, in my dream in 1980. I do not claim any connections between the two, although some may exist on other than conscious levels.

SESSION FOUR

SCIENCE AND SCIENCE'S PICTURE. DESIRE AS ACTION.

AUGUST 18, 1980
9:10 P.M., MONDAY

(I sneezed three times just as Jane took off her glasses and went into trance. As Seth, she stared at me with quite an amused air, waiting until I was ready to take notes.)

Good evening.

("Good evening, Seth.")

Now: I want to begin by mentioning one of the most important and vital messages in your glass-door dream *(of two days ago),*[1] for its truth applies to the magical approach as well.

That is, the dream was giving you an example of one of the main characteristics of what we will call the magical approach. Ruburt did not stress this in his interpretation, which was otherwise excellent.

The main issue was the relative ease with which you were able to enlarge the hole in the glass door. Ease is the key word. To the world of the intellect, a glass door must be considered solid, as it is in the world of physical senses. In other quite as factual terms, indeed in the larger framework of facts, the door of course is not solid at all, as no objects are. Obviously that is known to science.

Science delegates the world of nature as the realm of <u>exterior</u> natural events. Its view of nature is therefore mechanistic. The natural self, however, like the rest of nature, possesses a rich dimension of inside psychological depth, that science, because of its own definitions, cannot perceive. Telepathy and clairvoyance, for example, are a part of natural effects, but they belong to a nature so much more expansive than science's definitions that they have been made to appear as highly unnatural eccentricities of behavior, rather than as natural components of consciousness.

(Pause.) It is also for that reason that they seem to fall outside of the realm of the s-a-n-e *(spelled)*. Such characteristics are, however, basic properties of the natural person. They do not appear very well under the auspices of the scientific method, because the scientific method is itself programmed to perceive only information that fits into its preconceived patterns. Such abilities appear to be unpredictable, discontinuous, only because you are so relatively <u>unaware</u> of what is actually quite constant psychological behavior. That is, such abilities operate so smoothly, so continuously, and with such ease *(intently)* that you become aware of them only under certain conditions. You are aware of what seem to be isolated hints of odd characteristics.

The intellect is basically able to handle many kinds of information, and information systems. It is far more flexible than you presently allow it to be. It can handle several *(pause)* main world views at once, realizing that they are each methods of perceiving and approaching reality. To some degree historically speaking, that sort of situation operated in the past when — comparatively speaking, now — people realized that there was indeed an inner world of complexity and richness that could be approached in certain fashions, one that existed alongside with the physical world, so that the two intersected. Certain approaches worked in one area, and others worked in the inner reality.

(9:29.) The intellect could handle both approaches, operating with separate assumptions. There were separate assumptions that applied to different realities. I do not mean to idealize those times. In so-called modern ages, however, the intellect has been stripped down, so to speak. Science perceived the spectacular complexity of exterior reality, but turned its sights completely away from any recognition — any at all — until it regarded subjectivity itself as a mere throw-away product, accidentally formed by a mindless matter.

All of this applies to your situation, for I want you to thoroughly understand, intellectually and emotionally, the errors of current thought, so that you can see that our material is indeed providing you not only with "creative material," but with a more factual presentation of the framework in which you have your existence.

In modern times, then, the intellect was finally left with only one acceptable world view, with one set of assumptions, with only one main approach to reality and experience. The acceptable assumptions to a large extent ran directly contradictory to built-in biological, spiritual, and psychological assumptions that are a part of man's heritage. The intellect does try to order experience, to make sense out of perception. When it is enriched (pause) by having in its possession several world views, then it does an excellent job of merging those into meaningful patterns, of sorting information and sending it to the proper places, so to speak.

It understands, for example, that clairvoyant material is a part of the personality's overall characteristics, so it is not afraid of perceiving it — and it is able to separate such information confusion from present physical sense perception. Orderliness, then, is one of its main characteristics. When it is given only one world view, and only one group of assumptions, its orderly nature causes it to throw out all information that does not fit. It is almost forced to make an orderly picture, say like a jigsaw puzzle picture, while being denied half of the pieces.

The intellect is not to blame. It does the best it can under those conditions.

Now in your dream, you were quite clearly seeing the threshold between physical reality and the magical dimension in which that physical reality has its source. You were being shown — or showing yourself — the difference in the rules or assumptions between the two. The dog's desire for food led him to walk magically through the door, for the desires of the natural creature are satisfied *(pause)* with an ease that has nothing to do with your ideas of work. What I am getting at is the introduction of the concepts of a different kind of work — very valuable, vital work that is performed at another level and in a different fashion.

(9:48.) A prime example, of course, is the "work" done to keep each and every creature alive and breathing, the "work" done to keep the planets in their places, the "work" being done so that one evolutionist can meditate over his theories.

Now in your dream you got the feeling of that kind of work, or action. It is the given power of the world, the given power of nature. It is the directed force of value fulfillment.[2] In other terms it is of course the energy of All That Is. The trouble is that the rational view of life has separated man from a sense of his own power source. When he has a problem, the rational approach to its solution seems the only answer, and often, of course, it is no answer at all.

Ruburt wanted to make sure that he was right. *(Long pause.)* He tried to go ahead and not go ahead at the same time. He tried to be daring and cautious, brave and safe. This applies to some extent to each of you, of course, precisely because you were gifted strongly both intellectually and intuitively. You tried to rationalize your creativity, both of you, to some extent. The rational line of thought finds creativity highly disruptive, so in those terms as highly gifted creative people, you would have encountered some difficulties in any case.

It is time that you regarded such difficulties instead as challenges that are a part of a creative adventure that you have yourselves chosen. You chose the adventure because it was the kind best suited to your own individual value fulfillment. In reconciling the many concepts and contradictions for yourselves, you also lead the way for many others. It would, again, help considerably if you thought of your work more as an adventure, an exciting creative adventure, than of work in your old terms.

This will allow you to include the feeling of inner, magical "work" into your calculations. It would also begin (underlined) to give you a feeling for the magical support that upholds you both, and your lives — the support that Ruburt can count upon, and that can bring about the solution to his physical difficulties. Here, again, the vital word is ease or effortlessness. If you want to *(long pause)* feed a dog in the physical world — and he is on the other side of the door — you must open it. In the inner world you or the dog can walk through the door without effort, because desire is action. Desire is action.

In the inner world, your desires bring about their own fulfillment, effortlessly. That inner world, and the exterior one, intersect and interweave. They only appear separate. *(Pause.)* In the physical world, time may have to elapse, or whatever. Conditions may have to change, or whatever, but the desire will bring about the proper results. The feeling of effortlessness is what is important. It is quite proper for Ruburt's intellect to understand this, and to say, simply now, "That is not my realm. I will leave the solution to that problem where it belongs. We will use the magical approach here."

If you want to, rest your fingers briefly.

(10:08. "Okay." Then at 10:09:)

Now, briefly: I will continue the above discussion at our next session.

Ruburt feels hopeless at times because the assumptions of the rational approach often lead in that direction, and because he has not been certain enough of himself in those other areas to get the kind of long-lasting results he wants. This applies to both of your attitudes at times.

At a conscious level, of course, neither of you realized, or wanted to realize, the kind of complete repeal and overhaul that was implied by our sessions, and for some years you managed to hold many official views of reality along with the newer concepts, not ready to understand that an entire new way of thinking was involved, a new relationship of the individual with reality. So you tried out some new methods piecemeal, here and there, with good-enough results.

Of course, an entire reorientation *(with emphasis)* is instead implied, and that entire reorientation will effortlessly bring about a new relationship of Ruburt with his body, with his life, and with the adventure the two of you have embarked upon. He will simply automatically get better, because the framework will allow him to do so.

A few mundane but helpful notes. He must of course be allowed some uninterrupted writing time. Neither of you understand your attitudes toward the bedroom. Both of you avoid making love in it. It is the one room that is not *(pause)* a part of your overall activities, of course. It seems isolated from your lives. You do not fix it up, for example. This is partially the result of old ideas, where sleep is a separate, isolated part of life, or of the personality.

You would both feel better in it if it showed more of your other interests. For Ruburt, some books or bookcases. It is a room that shows no evidence of his work, you see. It should hold some of your current paintings — but in some way it should be tied in with your lives more.

Ideally, a new bed would be advantageous, both physically and symbolically. Relaxation — laying down, for example — would be far more easily assimilated on Ruburt's part, also, if a cot or equivalent — a daybed or whatever — were a part of his writing room, or in the breezeway.

You enjoy the living room for a nap because of its sensual reaches. Your metabolisms are different, quite naturally, and under the usual situations, given your lunch hour, Ruburt needs a good meal, sometimes certainly between five and six at the latest. Otherwise he experiences a natural physical irritation that is complicated then by other issues. You need your painting time, as you have discovered. He enjoys the twilight hour in his writing room, and though the seasons have something to do with that, still it is a good idea when possible. Your own reassurances are very helpful — and remember that they operate on other than physical terms.

Now I bid you a fond good evening, and my congratulations to your fingers.

("They're okay.")

Good evening.

("Thank you. Good night, Seth.")

(10:29 P.M.)

NOTES: SESSION OF AUGUST 18, 1980

1. From my dream notebook: (See my painting at end of Session 4.)
"Dream, very early Saturday morning, August 16, 1980.

"I'll try to remember all elements of this dream in sequence. Most unusual. All in brilliant color:

"I dreamed that I was in the kitchen of the hill house, in Elmira, crouched down just inside the room's glass storm door, which was closed. The kitchen's inside wooden door was wide open, just to my left. Gus, the friendly old Shetland sheepdog who belonged to our neighbors across the street, came up to the storm door, looking for the handful of dry food I give him each morning when I scatter birdseed in the driveway. Gus was on the other side of the door, on the screened-in back porch, as he should be — only then I saw to my amazement that he was starting to walk <u>through</u> the glass panel in his eagerness to get to the food. I felt his head pushing effortlessly through the glass, and exclaimed about this to Jane, who sat at her usual place at the breakfast table just in back of me. I was really surprised. I had my hands on Gus's head as he sought to enter the kitchen through the glass.

"I gently pushed against Gus's head, and he began to back out through the glass. With a sudden inspiration I kept my hands on his head until they went through the glass with him as he withdrew. Then, in order to obtain some physical proof that this was really happening, with my right hand I began to 'carve' a squarish hole a few inches across in the glass where Gus's head had been. I made the opening as the glass began to 'congeal'. The hole's sides were smoothly rounded and posed no problem as far as sharp edges went. And I ended up with the proof I wanted — an irregular hole that I had formed in the glass with my fingers. The dream glass was about one-quarter-inch thick — double, say, its 'real' thickness.

"After the Gus part of the dream, I saw through the glass door a man standing quite at military attention. He was older, graying, impeccably dressed in the dark blue uniform of an officer of the Navy. He was handsome and tall and slim. He looked something like the blue male I'm painting from a recent dream, although that one is in civilian clothes. There's a resemblance between the two, but I'm not particularly claiming that the officer is the civilian. I only want to note that this would make the second instance recently in which I might have had the same character appear in separate dreams.

"The Navy man never came through the door like Gus had, though, nor did he speak to me or move. He simply stood at attention on the porch, symbolizing I don't know what. He was an officer of considerable rank, with a number of stripes on his cuffs. Perhaps the equivalent of an army colonel.

"Later in the dream, maybe at night, I was sitting on a couch with some close friends, as at a small party. My brother Linden, from out of town, could have been there. The room didn't look much like our living room at the hill house. Jane was present. I believe we had the TV on. Either a character on the screen said something, or someone in the room did — whatever, it triggered my memory of the Gus episode. I began to laugh and squirm with glee, telling our friends that I'd experienced something great, and that I could show them the physical evidence of it. I didn't get to actually show the hole in the glass, though, but for some little time I kept laughing and saying, to everyone's surprise and amusement, that I'd really had that adventure this morning."

Jane interpreted the dream the same day I had it:
"Dream of August 16, Saturday 1980 — the hand thru glass dream.

"This is another terrific dream, continuing the one in the last session, in which Rob was constructing an image of the magical self — seeing it as a kind of Captain Marvel character. In this dream, though, he uses the magic himself, making it far more accessible.

"The dream takes place in the kitchen, a room devoted to physical nourishment. Gus, the neighbors' dog, in an intense desire to get the food Rob holds, walks right through the glass door — signifying the importance of desire in bringing about the magical satisfaction of needs.

Gus probably also represents the 'creature' magical self, showing its creature characteristics; that it's natural, after all.

"At the same time, it's Rob's usual self, learning from the creature-magical self, who then 'gets the evidence,' enlarges the magical hole in the glass; signifying two things — that the so-called usual consciousness can learn from the magical part, follow its lead and therefore catch itself 'performing miracles.'

"Later in the dream Rob is reminded of this incident by something someone says, either on TV or in the room — signifying a different mobility of consciousness, almost a dream within a dream, and also establishing the fact that physical and magical events are related.

"I'm not quite sure of the meaning of the older handsome Navy man who stands at attention — an authority figure . . . whose purpose is merely to stand guard and observe; perhaps a reassurance to Rob that the rational self is there, in its true position — but standing apart, observing the magical proceedings. . . ."

Jane did such a fine job interpreting the dream (in my estimation!) that I didn't bug her for more details. Later, however, I wished that I'd asked her a few questions. I think she's quite right about the naval officer being a symbol for the more conventional, or rigid, rational self. I would have liked my wife's comments on my brother Linden being in the dream. He's a year younger than I am, and lives with his family down in Pennsylvania. He's become quite religiously oriented, as is his right. I think that as I joyfully talked about my magical exploration in the dream, I was telling him something like: "Hey, there's more than one way to explore the self, to be religious!" And I think that Linden and I were in correspondence in the dream state, and that in some way he got the message. . . .

2. According to Jane and Seth, within our time scheme each physically-endowed consciousness, whatever its form or size or complexity, inherently seeks to fulfill its own highest potential — not only for itself, but for the benefit of each other such consciousness in our reality.

There is no drifting through life, then, but a built-in search for the fulfillment of values, whatever possible successes, conflicts, or failures may
be involved, and no matter how modest or great or complex any of
those qualities may be. The ecstasy and love of being always operate to
ensure the quality and growth of life's existence through value fulfillment.

Robert F. Butts (1919–): *My Glass-Door Dream*. 1980. Oil on panel, 13 x 11 in.

My dream of August 16 was difficult to visually present: How could I show my contact with Gus through the seemingly solid glass — show that, as Seth says, desire is action? I first sketched the dream late in August, but didn't finish the painting of it until December.

SESSION FIVE

STYLES OF THOUGHT. COMBINING THE MAGICAL APPROACH
AND THE SO-CALLED RATIONAL APPROACH.

AUGUST 20, 1980
9:08 PM., WEDNESDAY

(We sat for the session at 8:45. Jane has been feeling considerably better: "My backside feels 75% better," she said again now. I'm back working on the chronology for Seth's latest book, Dreams, and have been doing some paintings involving my own dreams. Jane has done excellent work interpreting the dreams; some of my nighttime excursions have resulted from these sessions on the magical approach.

(Whispering.) Good evening.

("Good evening Seth.")

A continuation of our discussion.

The scientific framework of reference has become equated with the term "rational thinking," to such an extent that any other <u>slant</u> of thought automatically seems to be irrational. Thought has become, in that regard, too specialized, prejudiced, and inflexible.

Now there are styles of thought. Each individual has his or her own style of thinking, a peculiar, rich, individual mixture (*pause*) of speculations, fantasies, (*pause*) idiocentric ways of using subjective

· 51 ·

and objective data. Science has so dominated the world of thought, however, that many nuances and areas once considered quite "rational" have become quite unrespectable. Science tries to stick to what it can prove.[1]

Unfortunately, it tends to set up a world view that is then based upon certain material only. You end up with separate disciplines: biology, psychology, physics, mathematics, and so forth, each with its own group of facts, jealously guarded, each providing its own world view: the world as seen through biology, or reality as seen through the eyes of physics.

There is no separate field that combines all of that information, or applies the facts of one discipline to the facts of another discipline, so overall, science, with its brand of rational thought, can offer no even, suggestive, hypothetical, comprehensive ideas of what reality is. It seems that each individual is in effect isolated in certain vital regards — given, say, a genetic heritage and a certain amount of unspecified energy with which to run the body's machinery *(intently)*. Intent, purpose, or desire do not apply in that picture.

The individual is, again, a stranger, almost an alien, in his or her own environment, in which he must struggle to survive, not only against the "uncaring" forces of the immediate environment, but against the genetic determinism. He must fight against his own body, overemphasize its susceptibility to built-in defects, diseases, and against a built-in time bomb, so to speak, when without warning extinction will arrive. Science does not stress the cooperative forces of nature. It glories in distinctions, specifications, and categories, and is quite blind, generally speaking, to the uniting forces that are of course every bit as real. Therefore, when I speak of the natural person being also the magical person, it is easy to transpose even that idea into more isolated terms than I intend.

(9:23.) It is not just that each person has his or her source in a "magical" dimension, from which his or her overall life emerges, but that the private source itself is a part of the very energy that upholds the entire planet and its inhabitants, and the overall construct that you understand as the universe.

Fields, or p-l-a-n-e-s *(spelled)* of interrelatedness connect all kinds of life, supporting it not through, say, just one system — a biological one or a spiritual one — but at every conceivable point of its existence. You are not just given so much energy, in those terms earlier mentioned. "New" energy is everywhere available. Again, there are no closed systems. Again, the environment is conscious and alive. There are constant communications between all portions of your body and all portions of the environment.

(Pause.) In your terms this means that you do not have to rely upon what you think of as your private resources alone. Basically (underlined), value fulfillment is one of the most important characteristics of existence, so that all things act individually and together in ways that best provide for the overall fulfillment of the entire construct.

You were born because you desired to be born. A plant comes to life for the same reason. You live in a different frame of reference than a plant, however: You have more choices available. You interact with nature differently. Your intellect is meant to help you make choices. It allows you to perceive certain probabilities within a physical time context. You use the intellect properly when it is allowed to perceive physical conditions as clearly as possible. Then it can make the most beneficial decisions as to what goals you want to achieve.

(Pause.) Those goals are usually conceptualized desires, and

once formed they act in a fashion like magnets, drawing from those vast fields of interrelatedness the kinds of conditions best suited to their fulfillment. The intellect alone cannot bring about the fulfillment of those goals. The intellect alone cannot bring about one motion of the body. It must count upon those other properties that it does indeed set into motion — that spontaneous array of inner complexity, that orderly magic. Period.

When the intellect is used properly, it thinks of a goal and automatically sets the body in motion toward it, and automatically arouses the other levels of communication unknown to it, so that all forces work together toward the achievement. Consider a hypothetical goal as a target. When properly used, the intellect imagines the target and imaginatively then attains it. If it were a physical target, the person would stand [bow and] arrow in hand, thinking only of hitting the bull's-eye, mentally concentrating upon it, making perhaps some learned gestures — proper footing or whatever — and the body's magical properties would do the rest.

When the intellect is improperly used, however, it is as if the intellect feels required to somehow know or personally direct all of those inner processes. When the erroneous belief systems and negativity connected with so-called rational reason apply, then it is as if our person sees the target, but instead of directing his attention to it he concentrates upon all of the different ways that his arrow could go wrong: It could fall to the left or the right, go too far or not far enough, break in the air, fall from his hand, or in multitudinous other ways betray his intent.

(9:52.) He has switched his attention from the target, of course, completely. He has projected upon the present event the picture of his fears, rather than the picture of his original intent.

His body, responding to his mental images and his thoughts, brings out actions that mirror his confusion.

In other words, the magical approach and the so-called rational one are to be combined in a certain fashion for best results. People sometimes write you, telling of their intent to make money — or rather, to have it. They concentrate upon money, so they say, and wait for it in full faith that it will be attracted to them because of their belief and concentration. They might do the point of power exercise,[2] for example. They may also, however, have quit their jobs, ignored impulses to find other work, or to take any rational approaches, and rely upon, say, the magical approach alone. This does not work either, of course.

As Ruburt uses the magical approach, and as you use it, you will see that it blends in perfectly with the rest of existence, inspires the intellect, inspires physical motion — for it activates physical properties.

I will continue describing the ways in which the two approaches work together. The main point I want to make is, however, the fact that your private source of power is a portion of that greater field of interrelatedness, in which your being is securely couched. It is not something you have to strain after. It was effortlessly yours at birth, and before, and it carries with it its own emotional and intuitive comprehensions — comprehensions that can indeed support you throughout all of your physical existence. If you understand that, then in a large manner many of your fears will jointly vanish.

(Now to my surprise, Seth answered a question or two I'd asked Jane earlier today to relay to Sue Watkins — material I could use in my chronology for Dreams. Sue had recently given me some information, and my latest questions are extensions of those.)

· 55 ·

Tam[3] made the decision several times, but early in the game he decided that the book *(Sue's "Conversations With Seth")* should feature illustrations. George [Rhoads] was passive in the arrangement. Elaboration does not seem necessary. You can have it if you want.

("Okay," I said. I meant I didn't need the elaboration, but Seth mistook my reply, evidently, to mean that I did want it:)

Tam wanted illustrations for a first book. When he read of George's sketches he instantly thought of illustrations. Sue, of course, wanted to do George a favor, to make up for old issues. There were other probabilities according to George's situation, so that the affair at least opened up the idea that George could do other work for Prentice if he needed money. This gave him a sense of reassurance.

That is all for this evening. I bid you a magical good evening again — and remember to look for hints and clues at all levels of your existence.

("Thank you, Seth. Good night."

(10:08 P.M. Even though it was a shorter session, Jane's delivery had often been intent and emphatic. A good session, I told her. It's the next night as I type the session, of course. Today I sent Sue a copy of a recent page of Seth's material on the intellect, and a list of the questions about George that Seth discussed above. I expect her answers to tally with Seth's.

(Jane spent more time than usual in bed today, laying down in between her working stints.)

NOTES: SESSION OF AUGUST 20, 1980

1. See Appendix C for Jane's material, written later.

2. Seth emphatically says: THE PRESENT IS THE POINT OF POWER. According to him, the point of power is where flesh and matter meet with spirit. That juncture embodies the actions and beliefs we choose to draw from all of our previous points of power. From our current present we project, for better or worse, those choices, plus any new ones we may decide upon, into each of the presents we'll be creating throughout the rest of our lives. The contents of our projections, then, are of supreme importance.

As Seth suggests, through even a five-minute exercise, in which we sit quietly and look about, we can become aware that the present is the point of power. In his exercise, we gently remind ourselves that we aren't at the mercy of our past beliefs unless we think we are. We have the full freedom to insert new creative goals in our point-of-power exercises. Next, we relax, to give our fresh suggestions time to begin working within us. Next, physically we make a simple gesture or act, no matter how modest, that is in line with our desires for the future. Periodically we repeat the exercise — but easily, without pressure, confident that we're doing well. Action is thought in physical motion, Seth tells us . . . .

In *The Nature of Personal Reality*, Seth deals extensively with the point of power, its exercises and meanings and benefits. See especially sessions 656-57 in Chapter 15.

3. Tam Mossman was the editor at Prentice-Hall for both Jane and Sue. *Conversations With Seth* is Sue's fine two-volume account of the ESP classes Jane held from September 1967 to February 1975. Tam's enthusiastic and intuitive help was always invaluable to Jane, ever since he encouraged her to publish her first book, *The Seth Material*, in 1970.

Artist George Rhoads also attended ESP class. To Seth, George and Jane and Sue and I are "counterparts" — entities psychically connected to each other, and to other men, women, and children alive now in this country and in others. The connections can be conscious, unconscious, or both. Many of us will never meet physically, but as a group all of us are exploring related lifetime themes in ways that no individual can do.

Obviously, some ESP class members met counterparts in class. But I know that I've also met a counterpart outside of class, and later in life: Laurel Lee Davies, the beautiful young lady from Iowa who's been my loving companion for some years now, following Jane's death in 1984. Laurel is helping greatly as we put *The Magical Approach* together. She is doing invaluable work as a research and editorial assistant; studying Jane's notebooks, journals, and poetry, and putting together material from those sources to be included in this book. She has also been working with and choosing the published and unpublished Seth sessions for *The Magical Approach.* Laurel moved here in 1985 with us having that job for her in mind. I feel that Laurel's and my relationship is a clear case in which a long-standing "unknown" counterpart connection came into our consciousnesses when we were ready for it to, and that eventually it led to our meeting. Laurel has been involved with Jane's, Seth's and my work since November of 1979, when she was 24 years old. Her boyfriend recommended *Seth Speaks* to her. Although he did not believe in metaphysical realities, he had heard the book was the best of it's kind, and they found it in a used-book store in Seattle, Washington. Lauren began writing to Jane and me in 1980 — while Seth was dictating *The Individual and the Nature of Mass Events* and Jane was writing her *God of Jane.* What interesting timing. . . .

Fore much more Seth material on the counterpart concept, see Session 732 and Appendix 25 in Volume II of *The "Unknown" Reality* (Published by Amber-Allen Publishing, Inc., San Rafael, CA).

SESSION SIX

ANIMALS AND REASONING.
THINGS BEYOND ONE'S CONTROL.

AUGUST 25, 1980
8:49 P.M., MONDAY

(*Jane continues to show improvements. But she's been bothered more than once lately by the contents of some of her mail — the letters of woe she attracts from readers who earnestly petition aid of various kinds from Seth and herself. Today the trigger was furnished by another letter from a lady who lives in Kentucky. She's lost both breasts from cancer, and has a host of other physical and emotional problems. I suggested Seth comment on Jane's reactions tonight. I also told Jane that her reactions were probably triggered at least in part because of her own vulnerable position, due to her personal challenges.*

(*Jane's "walking" has improved much in the last week, especially, and overall since Seth began this series of personal sessions. She now can take, say, ten steps at a time, leaning on her typing table, instead of the one or two previously possible. But we've also grown careless again: She walks but once a day, instead of the twice I suggested recently, and which she agreed to, and which Seth seconded in a recent session. Still, we're very pleased with her progress.*

(*We sat for the session at 8:40. The evening was another beautiful one: It was dark already, with the hordes of cicadas and other insects sounding off in rhythmic chorus. Their music echoed through the nearby woods.*

(Whispering:) Now —

("Good evening.")

— good evening.

(With many pauses:) Part of the difficulty arises from the current *(pause)* scientifically-oriented blend of rationalism. It lies in the way in which the individual is defined. As a species, you think of yourselves *(pause)* as the "pinnacle" end of an evolutionary scale, as if all other entities from the first cell onward somehow existed in a steady line of progression, culminating with animals, and finally with man the <u>reasoning</u> animal. (In parentheses: with all of that progress occurring of course by chance, incidentally.)

New sentence: That particular blend of rational thinking with which your society is familiar takes it more or less for granted, then, that man's identity as a species, and the identity of the individual, is first and foremost connected with the intellect. You identify yourselves with your intellect, primarily, casting aside as much as possible other equally vital elements of your personhood.

New sentence: In your historical past, when man identified his identity with the soul, he actually gave himself greater leeway in terms of psychological mobility, but eventually the concept of the soul as held resulted in a distrust of the intellect. *(Pause.)* That result was the inevitable follow-up of dogma. Period. Part of man's latest over-identification with the intellect is, of course, an overreaction to those past historical events. Neither religion or science grant other creatures much subjective dimension, however: You like to think of yourselves, again, as the reasoning animal in terms of your species.

(9:01.) However, animals do reason. They do not reason in the same areas that you do *(intently)*. In those areas in which they do reason, they understand cause and effect quite well. Their reasoning is applied, however, to levels of activity to which your own reasoning is not applied. Therefore, often animal reasoning is not apparent to you. Animals are curious. Their curiosity is applied to areas in which you seldom apply your own.

The animals possess a consciousness of self, and without the human intellect. You do not need a human intellect to be aware of your own consciousness. Animals, it is true, do not reflect upon the nature of their own identities as man does *(pause)*, but this is because that nature is intuitively comprehended. It is self-evident.

I only want to show you that the sense of identity need not inevitably be coupled with the intellect exclusively. Your intellect is a part of you — a vital, functioning portion of your cognitive processes — but it does not contain (underlined) your identity.

(Long pause at 9:10.) The natural person is understood perhaps more clearly by considering any person as a child. In a fashion the child discovers its own intellect, as it discovers its own feelings. Feelings come "first." The child's feelings give rise to curiosity, to thoughts, to the operation of the intellect: "Why do I feel thus and so? Why is grass soft, and rock hard? Why does a gentle touch soothe me, while a slap hurts me?"

The feelings and sensations give rise to the questions, to the thoughts, to the intellect. The child in a fashion feels — feels — its own thoughts rise from a relative psychological invisibility into immediate, vital formation. There is a process there that you have forgotten. The child identifies with its own psychic reality first of all — then discovers its feelings, and claims those, and discovers its thoughts and intellect, and claims those *(all quite intently)*.

The child first explores the components of its psychological environment, the inside stuff of subjective knowledge, and claims that inner territory, but the child does not identify its basic being with either its feelings or its thoughts. That is why, for example, it often seems that young children can die so easily. *(Still intently):* They can disentangle themselves because they have not as yet identified their basic beings with life experience. Period.

In most cases children grow up, of course *(pause)*, although in the vast overall picture of nature *(pause)* a goodly proportion of individuals do indeed take other courses. They serve other functions, they have other purposes, they take part in life through a different cast of action. They affect life while themselves not completely immersed in it. They die young. They are aborted. They remain, however, an important element in life's overall picture — part of a psychological underpainting that always affects later versions.

Ideally, however, children finally claim their feelings and their thoughts as their own. They identify naturally with both, finding each valid and vital. By the time you are an adult, however, you have been taught to disconnect your identity from your feelings as much as possible, and to think of your personhood in terms of your intellectual orientation. Your identity seems to be in your head. Your feelings and your mental activity therefore appear, often, quite contradictory. You try to solve all problems through the use of reasoning alone.

(9:27.) You are taught to submerge the very intuitive abilities that the intellect needs to do its proper work — for the intellect must check with the feeling portions of the self for feedback, for support, for knowledge as to biological conditions. Denied that feedback, it can spin on endlessly in frenzied dry runs. *(Long*

pause.) At each moment, from the most microscopic levels the body *(pause)* in one way or another is ascertaining a constant picture of its position within physical reality. That picture is composed of millions of ever-changing smaller snapshots, as it were — or moving pictures is better — determining so many conditions, positions and relationships that they could never be described. You end up with a predominating picture of reality in any given moment — one that is the result of the activity of psychological, biological, and electromagnetic stratas. One picture is transposed upon the others, and calculations made constantly, so that all of the components that make up physical existence are met, and intersect to give you life.

None of that is the intellect's concern at an intellectual level. At a biological level, and at an electromagnetic level, the intellect, of course, performs feats that it cannot consciously know through the use of its reason *(all intently)*. Spontaneously, with the process just mentioned, millions of pictures are being taken also of the probable actions that will — or <u>may</u> — be needed, in your terms, in the moment immediately following, from microscopic action to the motion of a muscle, the driving of a car, the reading of a book, or whatever.

One of the intellect's main purposes is to give you a conscious choice in a world of probabilities. To do that properly the intellect is to make clear, concise decisions, on its level, of matters that are <u>its</u> concern, and therefore to present its own picture of reality to add to the entire construct. *(Long pause.)* On the one hand you have been told to identify yourselves almost completely with your intellects. On the other hand, you have been taught that the intellect, the "flower of consciousness," is a <u>frail</u>, vulnerable adjunct — again, a chance creation, without meaning and without support

— without support because you believe that "beneath it" lie "primitive, animalistic, bloody instincts," against which reason must exert what strength it has.

(9:46.) Despite all of that, men and women still find the solutions to many of their problems by rediscovering the larger sense of identity[1] — a sense of identity that accepts the intuitions and the feelings, the dreams and the magic hopes as vital characteristics, not adjuncts, of personhood. When I tell you to remember your own natural persons, I do then want to remind you not to identify with your intellects alone, but to enlarge your scopes of identity. Automatically those other, often-shunted-aside characteristics begin to add their richness, fulfillment, and vitality to your lives effortlessly.

(9:50.) Now give us a moment.

(Pause.) With Ruburt: The new orientation is bringing results, and the results do appear effortlessly.[2] The affair with Mitzi *(one of our cats)* did involve action at other levels — a magical orientation. Ruburt is doing well. Have him remember that creative activity goes on within him all of the time, and he is often most active precisely when he is not aware of it. He is only aware of those moments when creative activity surges into his conscious awareness, and by then much of the "work" has already been done.

He is not responsible for other people's realities, but he is responsible for his own. Give us a moment . . . .*(Pause, eyes closed).* The ill woman's reality does not threaten his own in any way. The situation, however, shows that he sometimes still thinks he should be able to solve all problems, and to know all the reasons for any given sorrow or tragedy. The intellect cannot handle that kind of information at that level.

Some answers come when you are ready for them. Then they

come naturally, as a matter of understanding and comprehension. The question of life's tragedies still cannot be answered satisfactorily at the level at which either of you — or anyone else — is currently asking it. I can give hints and clues and explanations that are quite valid within that context *(intently)*. *(Long pause.)*

As a matter of fact, the kind of literal answers that you may think you want can indeed lead you somewhat astray in terms of the larger picture, so Ruburt must say: "That is not my province," send energy, a note now and then; but the particular problem, the specific problem is the woman's, not Ruburt's.

The reason for the problem is a philosophical concern of Ruburt's, and of yours, but it is one whose answer — or answers — will gradually unfold. All of this information I consider necessary, again, to provide an overall atmosphere of comprehension that will allow the release of your own vitalities and strengths in an effortless manner, in such a way that your own problems begin to dissolve.

The kind of orientation I am speaking of represents the truest picture I can give you of man's natural relationship with himself and the world. This is how it works. This is physical.

End of session — and again, a magical good evening.

("Thank you, Seth. Good night.")

(10:07 P.M. I told Jane that if Seth hadn't gone into it on his own, I'd have asked him to comment on her mail reactions. Jane said she'd also wanted material on the mail; she seldom asks for anything specific from Seth before a session. I told her she'd done well.

(About Seth's reference to Mitzi: Last month both of our cats, Mitzi and Billy, came down with heavy cases of fleas — quite unusual for them even though they are often outside. I bought flea collars, and got one on Billy without trouble. When I tried to slip the other one over Mitzi's head,

though, I ran into a hornet's nest of resistance, and Jane couldn't help. Mitzi actively avoided us for many days before we could make friends anew with her.

(Last Saturday, on the 23rd, I bought another pair of flea collars. Mitzi in the meantime had become thoroughly miserable, and I had determined that I was going to get a collar on her somehow. A friend had suggested using a towel to prevent her scratching. When I set out to do the job that afternoon, Jane suggested using catnip on the towel. After some coaxing on the back porch, I got Mitzi rolling around in the catnip on the towel, but only half succeeded in wrapping her up. I carried her squirming into the kitchen. Jane was doing the dishes. I knelt on the floor holding the cat, while Jane mentally tried to soothe her struggles — and I succeeded in getting the flea collar in place around her neck. Actually, Mitzi didn't resist half as much as I'd feared she would. I'd thought I might totally alienate her this time if she fought too hard, but such was not the case. Jane said she'd sent Mitzi a stream of suggestions while I coaxed her into letting me put the collar on her. Everything worked well. I fed her a few times that afternoon, and succeeded in making friends okay. Mitzi hasn't tried to get the collar off. It has a medicinal smell. Now, several days later — as I type this session on Wednesday night — she seems to feel much better.)

Notes: Session of August 25, 1980

1. See Appendix D.

2. Jane wrote these notes in her journal last Sunday, the day before she delivered this session on August 25 — but I present them here to show how, from her own perspective, she very nicely covers events I too wrote about in connection with the session.

"Sunday, August 24, 1980.

"Yesterday walked with the typing table still further, the full length of the kitchen. Again, this represents the best improvement in that area since last winter . . .

"Anyhow, have been applying the Magical Approach to a variety of other areas, household annoyances, with some gratifying results. Mitzi, our cat, has been loaded with fleas. Rob tried to get a collar on her a month ago and there was such a hassle, he gave up, got mad at the cat, and vice versa. Yesterday he tried again, both of us remembering the Magical Approach; me saying mentally that the affair would take place easily, etc. Rob did get the thing on the cat with much less difficulty; she didn't even seem to resent it. Granted, this might have happened anyhow. The point is that the odds didn't seem to go in that direction and that I do think . . . we did mental work at other levels that resulted in that benign event . . . as if before we gave cluttered orders for an event to take place.

"Several aches or whatever in various parts of my body came and vanished as I used this approach . . . where before that sort of thing used to last longer. Have been very relaxed; still lay down two or three times a day — do notes, read, rest . . . yesterday wrote letter to the editor about my mention in the 'miracle' article in [the well-known] psychology magazine.

"Later 8/24/80

"Again, walk a bit further, and this time after my shower my back isn't any worse. The problem is caused by sitting down so much — the pressure, and the heat and humidity. Answered 35 letters over the weekend . . . my mood seems again magically improved at least. Finished letter to the magazine; it gets mailed Monday A.M."

SESSION SEVEN

The Intellect as a Cultural Artifact. Creating One's Own Experience.

AUGUST 28, 1980
8:37 P.M., THURSDAY

(Jane was so uncomfortable from the hot and humid weather last night that she didn't hold the regularly scheduled session. The temperature reached 94 degrees yesterday; at bedtime it was still 75, with a humidity of 68%. It's the latter that she reacts to the most, it seems from my viewpoint. She promised a "short session" for this evening. I've often hesitated to mention it, but as I did remark a few days ago, I feel her reaction to the weather must have other causes — that is, besides those having to do with simple environmental conditions. As it is, life within the environment becomes difficult. Nor am I discussing living in an "ideal" environment all the time.

(Today has been much cooler. I was almost chilly in my cutoffs as we sat for the session at 8:30. Jane has felt much better. Her walking continues to improve, as well as her anatomy generally. She's succeeded very well in maintaining steady improvements that are most heartening to us both.

(Seth comments on weather tonight. He began the session very quietly, and took many pauses, including a number of long ones, as the session progressed.)

Good evening.

("Good evening, Seth.")

Now: The intellect is far more socially oriented than is generally understood.

Some of this, again, is difficult to explain *(pause)*, but in a fashion the intellect is a <u>cultural</u> (underlined) phenomenon. Period. It is amazingly resilient, in that according to the belief structures of any given historical period, it can orient itself along the lines of those beliefs, using all of its reasoning abilities to bring such a world picture into focus, collecting data that agree, and rejecting what does not.

Obviously, the mind can use its reasoning abilities, for example, to come to the conclusion that there is a single god behind the functioning of the world, that there are many gods, that divinity is a fantasy, and that the world itself springs from <u>no</u> reasonable source. New sentence: Like statistics, the reasoning abilities can be used to come to almost any conclusion. This is done, again, by taking into consideration within any given system of reasoning only the evidence that agrees with the system's premises.

This flexibility allows the species great variation overall in its psychological and cultural and political and religious activities. *(Long pause.)* When any system of reasoning becomes too rigid, however, there are always adjustments made that will allow other information to intrude — otherwise, of course, your belief systems would never change.

Your species shares with the other species a feeling of kinship for its kind. There is a great give-and-take of ideas. You end up, then, with a consensus, generally speaking, as to what a reasonable picture of agreed-upon reality is. Your system has frowned upon many experiences, considering them eccentric behavior in an adverse fashion, since your belief systems have so regimented behavior, and so narrowly defined sanity. *(Long pause.)* The intellect, I want to stress, is socially oriented. It is peculiarly suited, of course, to react to cultural information. *(Pause.)* It wants to see the world as it is seen by the minds of others. Through that kind of action it helps form your cultural environment, the civilization of which you are justly proud.

(8:54.) The intellect, then, helps your species translate its own natural purposes and intents — the purposes and intents of the natural person — into their "proper" cultural context, so that those abilities the natural person possesses can benefit the civilization of its time. Those purposes and intents literally change the world. The intellect's expectations and intents spontaneously and automatically trigger the proper bodily mechanisms to bring about the necessary environmental interactions, and your intent as expressed through your intellect directs your experience of the world.

I am speaking about the intellect here for our discussion, but remember it is everywhere cushioned also. There are backup systems, in other words *(amused)*. If the intellect believes that the world *(pause)* is a threat to existence, then that belief will alter its intents, of course, and therefore the body's activities. The beliefs of the intellect operate then as powerful suggestions, particularly when the intellect identifies with those beliefs, so that there is little distance between the intellect and the beliefs that it holds as true.

(Pause in an intent delivery.) I am doing my best to explain the very practical aspects of the intellect's beliefs, and their strength in drawing experience to you. At one time you both had difficulty with understanding some of these ideas. *(Pause.)* Your own relationship, your private beliefs about the sort of persons you wanted

individually for mates, brought about incalculable actions that led finally to your meeting — yet it all happened "quite naturally," of course. Your beliefs bring you into correspondence with the elements likely to lead to their affirmation. They draw from Framework 2 all of the necessary ingredients. They elicit from other people behavior that is in keeping with those beliefs.

Your own attitudes, for example — and beliefs — about foreigners, Prentice-Hall, people's stupidity and lack of integrity, put you in correspondence with those same beliefs on the part of others, resulting in the translation fiasco.[1] An entirely different kind of behavior could have been elicited from those same people. Like attracts like in that regard. Those same people, for example, all have, as you do, beliefs in people's trustworthiness, and so forth — but under those conditions, at that time, you each — or rather you all — were in correspondence at many levels. The books were published. They have helped many people, and that is because you were also in correspondence as far as many of your more positive beliefs are concerned, and those did outweigh the others.

You get what you concentrate upon, and your beliefs are largely responsible for those areas in which you concentrate.

(9:14.) There are no magical methods, only natural ones that you use all of the time, although in some cases you use them for beliefs that you take for truths, when instead they are quite defective assumptions. A small example — one, incidentally, that Ruburt finally realized; but it is a beautiful instance of natural methods. He used it beautifully, even though the results were not pleasing at first. It also shows Ruburt's growing understanding:

He heard tomorrow's weather report *(yesterday)*, groaned, thought of a very uncomfortable 90-degree temperature tomorrow [and] imagined himself miserable with the heat. Indeed, he began to feel warmer. In a flash he remembered previous days of discomfort, and in the next moment he projected those into the weekend. He felt trapped. Midway through this process he tried to catch himself, but he believed that his body could not handle the heat — and that belief outweighed his intent to change his thoughts, so they kept returning for perhaps ten minutes.

He continued, however, to remind himself that he was not going to worry about tomorrow today, regardless. He told himself that the prediction might be wrong, and he began with his intellect to pile up evidence that could in one way or another bring about a different, more beneficial experience. He did this by recognizing the way he had earlier been building up the picture in the old manner, by collecting all the evidence that fitted it. He used the same process, only for a more beneficial picture, and the process works. You have only to become aware of it.

Your experience will follow your concentration and belief and expectation. The mind is a great discriminator. It can use its reasoning to bring about almost any possible experience within your framework.

Now: Ruburt's body is definitely recovering normal motion. Laying down is excellent. The additional moving about, however, from one place to another, is most beneficial. The sensations in his buttocks of heat, even burning at times, and in the legs and feet, all represent additional motion and beneficial activity. Sometimes at night the activity might make him feel uncomfortable, but the body is activating itself in certain ways while it is supported.

Have him write a poem a day, and do an ink sketch. The thought came to him. It is a good one, while mind and body both relax.

(With some amusement:) I think that your painting of the dog is excellent.

("Thank you.")

I am not an artist, but I know what I like as much as anyone else does.

End of session, with one point: These changes in Ruburt's body are as magical as any precognitive dream in that regard.

A fond good evening,

("Thank you, Seth. The same to you. Good night."

(9:30 P.M. The session had been a relatively short one after all. I told Jane it was very good. Seth referred to the painting I'm working on of my dream of last August 16, — the one in which I'm kneeling at the kitchen storm door and thrusting my hand through the glass to touch Gus, the dog who belongs to our neighbors across the street. Seth and Jane have both analyzed this excellent dream.[2] Today I'd shown Jane how far I've progressed with a charcoal drawing based upon the dream, with a little preliminary color added to some parts of it.

(The theme of the dream had interested me pictorially from the beginning, I told her, but I'd almost lacked the nerve to try a rendition of it in paint. Late last week I started the charcoal drawing for the painting, however, figuring I could only try to see what I could do. . . So far, so good.)

NOTES: SESSION OF AUGUST 28, 1980

1. In October 1979 Jane and I saw, to our dismay, that the Dutch publisher of the translation of *Seth Speaks* had violated his contract with Prentice-Hall by making many unauthorized cuts in the book. It was supposed to be published in its entirety, but language difficulties led to the mixup. After hearing from Jane and me and her editor, Tam Mossman, the Dutch publisher agreed to market a new, uncut

translation of *Seth Speaks* this year. This will be an expensive undertaking
— one we feel bad about now that our initial anger has passed.

2. See Note 1 for the session of August 18.

SESSION EIGHT

NATURE AS MAN'S CARETAKER.
NATURAL MAGICAL REASONING AND TRUST.

SEPTEMBER 3, 1980
8:55 P.M., WEDNESDAY

(J ane didn't hold a session last Monday night. She was too relaxed. At the same time she was experiencing so many beneficial bodily changes that she didn't feel like concentrating. The evening was also quite hot and humid — with the temperature over 80 degrees at session time — and this bothered her considerably. "I'm just having one tonight because I didn't on Monday," she said.

(Her physical improvements continue in the overall way that Seth said they would. This morning I noticed a good improvement in the movement of Jane's knees over what they were capable of, say, a month ago. Her lower legs swing back and forth perhaps four inches, so changes in the knee joints have occurred. Her walking is still better than it was. She rests in bed mid-morning and mid-afternoon for a half hour or so, working part of the time on notes, poetry, etc.

(I'm busy figuring out various chronologies to use as background and reference material in my notes for Seth's next book, Dreams, "Evolution," and Value Fulfillment. *Today I worked also on chronologies for a Dutch publisher, and for the film producer who's optioned the movie rights to*

Jane's Oversoul Seven *novels.*

(Whispering:) Good evening.

(Whispering: "Good evening, Seth.")

Now *(pause)*: Man likes to think of himself as the caretaker of nature and the world. It is closer to the <u>truth</u>, however, to say — in that regard, at least — that nature is <u>man's</u> caretaker; or that man exists, physically speaking, as the result of the graceful support of nature and all of its other species. Without those other species, man as you know him would not exist, not without the continuous cooperation of those species with each other, and their interrelationships with the environment.

(Pause.) Man serves his purposes within nature, as all species do, and in the terms of your understanding man "thinks" in his own way, but he is also the thinking portion of nature. He is the portion that thinks, in your understanding, again, of that term.

(9:01.) Give us a moment. . . He deals with the effect of thinking upon nature, so to speak. He adds to the rest of nature. *(Pause.)* He therefore adds a different kind of mental organization — an organization, then, that nature itself requires, anticipates, and desires. Animals do not read or write books, but they do "read" nature directly through the context of their own experience, and through intuitive knowing. Man's reasoning mind adds an <u>atmosphere</u> to nature *(pause)*, that is as real, say, as the Van Allen Belts *(or radiation fields)* that surround the earth.

The thinking mind to a large degree directs the activity of great spontaneous forces, [with] energy-cellular organization being, say, the captain *(pause)* of the body's great energy sources. The reasoning mind defines, makes judgments, deals with the physical objects of the world, and also with the cultural interpretations current in its time.

Think of your own government in ideal terms for a moment. Its citizens are all individuals, with their own lives and interests. The government, if it has their loyalty, utilizes their energies in such a fashion that the majority are benefited, as is the government itself. Yet you cannot really put your finger on "the government," though you might mention the White House as the seat of its power. The government is composed of many people, of course, and really extends all the way down the line, even to its least citizen, but the government can direct the use of energies, of goods, commerce, power, and so forth.

The people count upon the government to realistically define the conditions of the world, to have proper intelligence so that the activities in foreign lands are known, to keep up proper communication with other governments, and so forth. Now in some important respects the reasoning mind is like the government in this analogy. If the people in power are paranoid, then they overestimate the dangers of any given world situation. They overreact, or overmobilize, using a disproportionate amount of energy and time for defense, and taking energies away from other projects. The reasoning mind acts in the same fashion when paranoid beliefs are in power. It therefore tells all of the citizens — or cells of the body — to mobilize for action, to be on the alert, to pare down all but necessary activities, and so forth.

When a government is paranoid, it even begins to cut down on the freedom of its own peoples, or to frown upon behavior that in freer times would be quite acceptable. The same applies to the conscious mind in that situation. Now the people might finally revolt, or they will take certain steps to see that their freedom is restored, and so the body's cells will do the same.

So what we want, obviously, is to ensure that the conscious

mind, with its reasoning processes, can make proper adjustments about the nature of the world and the individual citizens within it. I will return later to the purposes of man's conscious mind in nature, and part of that discussion will fall in our book *(Dreams).*

(9:25.) Man's mind is really more of a process. It is not a completed thing, like an arm or leg, but a relationship and a process. That process has its source in what I can only call *(pause)* "natural reasoning."

You are given far more knowledge than you realize when you are born, for example. I am not speaking of genetic information alone, as you understand it, but of a natural (underlined) yet intuitive reasoning process that is the result of the relationships that exist among all portions of the body. This is the kind of "reasoning" that is the source from which thinking emerges, and you might think of it as magical reasoning.

Each creature is born trusting *(quietly in an intent delivery).*

There is no such thing as a killer instinct, with the implications and meaning that man gives that term *(intently).* At levels almost impossible to describe to you in your adulthoods, all infants, for example, know that they are born into the environmental niches that suit them and no others — [that are] tailored to their requirements. You can usually see in a superficial fashion how animals under "natural conditions" fit into their environments so perfectly, so that their needs and desires and equipment meet and merge with the characteristics of the environment. It is not nearly as easy to see that the same applies to man and his mental and physical environment, his town or country or culture, but the infant trusts from the very first moment.

You may not consider trust an attribute connected with reasoning, but it is indeed, for it represents the creature's innate understanding of the support with which it has been gifted. The natural person still feels that trust. There are many books written about occult knowledge, or magical knowledge. Most of them are filled with distortions, but they are all efforts to uncover man's natural magical reasoning. I will also have more to say on that subject later.

Now: Had Ruburt gone to a doctor or a faith healer when we began our last group of sessions, and then in a matter of a week or so found himself able again to walk with his [typing] table across the kitchen floor, some thirteen or fourteen steps perhaps, where before three were his uncomfortable limit, he might have attributed the improvement to a doctor's treatment or to a faith healer's ability — but he would have been impressed. He would have been impressed also with the greater obvious motion of his feet, the feelings of release in the legs now spreading to the back and shoulders.

Those improvements came about in their way magically, because he has begun to use and understand this material. So let him be just as impressed — in fact, more impressed — at the body's natural healing processes, that will naturally flow and are naturally flowing when he allows himself to trust his life and the support of his own being.

Work with the sessions of late. For again, it is your understanding that sets it all into motion. There are changes in the hips occurring, and remarkable improvements already "in the works." They must be allowed to happen, however, and that takes place as your understanding brings you in greater correspondence with the natural energy that is always your own.

(Pause.) I bid you a fond — and again, magical — good evening.

("Thank you very much." Pause. "Good night."

(9:48 P.M. For several seconds Seth and I stared at each other with some amusement. After she came out of trance Jane told me that she had picked up from Seth that he liked the way my painting of "the dog" — Gus, from my dream of August 16 — was coming. I finished the thin under-painting for it this morning and must now wait a few days for it to dry. In the meantime I'm going back to work on my impressionistic tree painting and the one of the dream man and boy in blue.)

SESSION NINE

THE BODY'S REASONING AS LOGIC. BELIEF SYSTEMS.

SEPTEMBER 8, 1980
8:43 P.M., MONDAY

("I just hope I can handle it," Jane said again. Meaning the session. "There's so much going on in my body at one time it's hard to handle that too," she laughed. She referred to the continuing series of changes — improvements — taking place all through her body. At the moment these involve definite extra mobility — and soreness and itching — in her ankles and feet, for example. Right now her arms look longer, straighter. Today she's been "pretty well out of it," while trying to help me get through the changes we want to make in the copy-edited Mass Events. She's helped a great deal here, writing the initial version of certain notes, which I'll then add to before returning the manuscript to Prentice-Hall for printing.

(She's also been quite restless in bed at night. When she wakes up she does exercises sometimes. I suggested she get up, but the exercises seem to substitute for the physical activity that getting up would entail.

(Jane yawned at 8:42: "I almost feel him around . . . I guess I'll try. . . ." She sipped wine and laughed. "I think it'll be short.")

Now: Good evening.

("Good evening, Seth.")

A brief session.

There has been one rather remarkable improvement in Ruburt's performance: getting to his feet. That is the result of the body's magical reasoning — for the body reasons so quickly, so clearly and concisely *(pause)*, that its deductions, its logic, are far too fast for the intellect to follow. The body reasons directly. The body's reasoning transforms itself into action, with nothing to stand between its elegant logic and the *(pause)* logic's brilliant execution. Ruburt could not possibly follow all of the manipulations necessary so that the recent improvements could take place. Again, bodily efforts are as magical, as creative, certainly, as the writing of a book or a poem *(intently)* — but Ruburt in the past trusted his creative abilities as if they were something he had to guard from his physical self.

You are both finally making vital strides in understanding as a result of our last sessions in particular, and on Ruburt's part because of the changed attitudes he has allowed, and the changed physical habits: the encouragement of motion, the expanded feeling of identity, which now includes the physical body rather than trying to exclude it.

The body is not a tool, to do your mental bidding. *(Pause.)* Your body is a mental expression physically materialized. More improvements are indeed even now occurring, and as long as Ruburt's attitude continues to improve you can expect such progress — for again, the body is quite capable of healing itself completely, and with far greater ease than you give it credit for.

Ruburt did not have to <u>do</u> anything in particular, for example, of a conscious nature, except to state his intentions, and the body's healing mechanisms immediately quickened. This is because he began to take the pressure off, so to speak, and really began to understand the abilities and limitations of the rational mind in its relationship to the body.

(8:59.) You both believed it was quite possible to have clairvoyant dreams, out-of-body experiences, creative adventures in the arts — but to some extent both of you doubted that the same power or energy could be directed effectively in the physical realm, so-called, of bodily health, or situations of the nitty-gritty *(with emphatic amusement)*. Again, the material is indeed dealing with a far more valid explanation for the working ways of reality than the old official beliefs — and again, we are not just (underlined) dealing with evocative, creative hypotheses.

There is no need, then, to be surprised if some of our ideas frighten Prentice-Hall.

("I was just going to ask you about that.")

If our ideas were already accepted in the world, there would be no need for our work. Prentice-Hall is, of course, well-intentioned, and under their belief system it is nearly sacrilegious to be anything more than officially disapproving of medical matters. That is, some disapproval is acceptable. To attack medical corruption, or medical errors, or particular clinics, for example, is within bounds, but to attack the belief system of the entire structure is something else again.

Their objections should simply show you why our work is so important. You must not forget, again, that you both chose these challenges. You wanted to be involved with the initiation of new thematic material. You wanted the experience of getting it for yourselves, so to speak *(intently)* — the exhilaration of discovery.

(Softly amused:) As a matter of fact — in case you may think sometimes that I am not fully aware of your mores — I did indeed temper many of my remarks in *Mass Events* on several subjects, so

that the book would not be found too objectionable in the context of your times. The implications are there, but your belief systems must be allowed to <u>mellow</u> and change in the light of new knowledge, rather than to be booted aside with an angry foot.

End of session, unless you have a question.

("No, I was just going to ask about Prentice-Hall.")

That is all I have to say there. They <u>are</u> a mainline publisher, which means that their books go to people in all walks of life — in libraries and bookstores and so forth. It is much better that the books compete in such a fashion with the other material of your times, rather than be published, say, by a specialty house, or coddled along the way, for we speak to all of those people.

Remember the last portion of this session, and your stomach need not bother you *(I laughed)* — or, more clearly, you will not need to bother your stomach, for that is the problem's secret.[1]

A fond good evening.

("Thank you very much, Seth. Good night."

(9:18 P.M. "I come out, and look at my eyes," Jane said half humorously. True, her eyes were relaxed into slits — although they gradually opened normally as we talked. "I'm glad I did that," she said, meaning that she'd held the session, "but I really didn't know whether I could. . . ."

(We laughed again when we considered that Seth had tempered some of his material for Mass Events. *"I'd hate to see it if he hadn't," Jane said.*

("I was so aware of my body today," she commented, "that I wondered if I'd be aware of it during the session, but all I remember is drinking wine — which is the kind of thing I usually remember."

(See the session for September 22 for our own ideas and feelings, and more of Seth's material, on the medical/disclaimer situation with Prentice-Hall.)

SESSION NINE

1. Seth is right, of course. As I well know, I *am* bothering my stomach, which is perfectly innocent in its own right. I've reacted to stress this way before. My stomach has been knotting up because I'm stewing over the reactions of those in charge at Prentice-Hall to Seth's material in *Mass Events* about medical matters.

My present uncomfortable state isn't drastic, by any means, but it is getting my attention — which, after all, is the reason I'm creating it to begin with. Maybe I'd be better off, I told Jane, if I'd just blow my top. Only who, or what, would I direct my frustration to, or at? On the one hand Jane, Seth, and I want to see our work presented to the world as originally conceived, as a way to offer ideas to think about. On the other hand, I can visualize the dilemma those at the publisher's feel when they're being asked to print ideas that are, at least in part, so contrary to accepted belief structures in a very important field. . . .

SESSION TEN

EDUCATION AND CULTURE. THE NATURAL PERSON.

SEPTEMBER 10, 1980
8:48 P.M., WEDNESDAY

*(A**t 8:30 this evening I finished typing Monday's short session [for the 8th]. I'd forgotten to do it last night, so absorbed was I in working on the copy-edited* Mass Events. *Then I made a surprising discovery as I put the session in private notebook number 23 — for there I found my original shorthand notes for the September 3 session. I'd also forgotten to type that one, and for the same reason, evidently. I believe that's the first time in well over a thousand sessions that I've forgotten to type one. I've deliberately let a few go for a while because I was busy on other things, but haven't simply forgotten any. Jane missed the September 3 session, but when she asked me about it a few days ago I replied that I was up to date. I remember wondering why she asked. . . .*

(Once again Jane was very relaxed as we prepared for the session. "I could go to bed right now," she said, "but it's too early — I'd be getting up all night. Right now I don't feel Seth around, though, but we'll see . . . My spine's got all kinds of feelings in it that I'm not used to, but they're good ones. How does Seth sit? I'm not sitting too well. I felt just great in bed this afternoon. There's a real fluid feeling there and in my back. But I

feel him around now. . . ." She sipped wine while I worked on these notes.

(Softly:) Now: Remarks.

(I nodded, smiling.)

Ruburt's body is repairing itself now at an excellent rate.

It is doing so because Ruburt is giving it different "orders." He is giving it a different picture of the world, and he is doing that because he has finally changed many of his old beliefs.

In actuality, the body's response to such information is always instantaneous, whether or not the results show at once. Ruburt is beginning to hold a more "realistic" picture of how overall reality works. He is managing to disentangle himself from many disadvantageous cultural beliefs — beliefs that both of you for years, like other people, took for granted.

You might <u>combat</u> those beliefs, struggle against them, but they still carried great weight. You still believed them to an important degree. The entire idea, or fear, that Ruburt had at one time of leading other people down the garden path, was based upon those old beliefs. Those ideas have vanished. You are approaching a state of mind, individually and jointly, that represents far more closely one that is natural, with which the natural person is innately equipped.

Education in your culture is a mixed bag *(with ironic and humorous emphasis)* — and education comes not from schools alone, but from newspapers and television, magazines and books, from art and from culture's own feedback. Generally speaking, for the purposes of this discussion, there are two kinds of education — one focused toward teaching the child to deal with the natural world, and one focused toward teaching the child how to deal with the cultural world. Obviously, these are usually combined. It is impossible to separate them.

Your educational systems, however, for all of their idealism, have largely ended up *(pause)* smothering the natural individual bents and leanings of children, and overemphasized instead the cultural organization. It became more important, then, for the child to conform to the culture rather than to follow its own individual natural leanings. Its own characteristic ways of dealing with nature were frowned upon, so that education does not work with the child's abilities, but against them. Education then often goes against the grain of the natural person.

(9:12.) This does not mean that some children do not do very well under your system. *(Pause.)* I do not mean to imply, either, that children do not need an education, or that some discipline and direction are not beneficial. Children, however, will concentrate for hours at a time on subject matters and questions that interest them. They are often taken from such pursuits, and their natural habits of concentration suffer as a result.

You are unlearning right now, and discovering that this particular unlearning process is indeed highly educational *(with emphasis)*. You are encountering your own natural knowledge.

(Pause.) In many instances, of course, you learned too well, both of you. The natural person that is yourself loved to draw and paint. You did that apart from what you had to do in school as a boy. You were lucky in your relationship with Miss Bowman.[1] Your talent brought you into correspondence with her. You can trust your natural inclinations. These sessions, in that regard, came naturally, as the expression of natural abilities and tendencies, finally emerging despite your official views at the time, jointly.

The sessions brought about, however, a new kind of education that often seemed in direct conflict with the old, and with the official views of contemporary society. It was of course necessary for you to test them out. Ruburt felt himself more responsible than you, since he spoke the words for me. A private search was one thing — but one publicly followed was something else *(intently).*

Whether or not the sessions happened as they did, however, once the two of you met, the probability brought about by your relationship meant that in one way or another you would seek out a larger context of consciousness — a context, because of your talents, that would not remain private, but attract others *(intently).*

(9:23.) The natural person is to be found, now, not in the past or in the present, but beneath layers and layers of official beliefs, so you are dealing with an archeology of beliefs to find the person who creates beliefs to begin with. As I have said often, evidence of clairvoyance, telepathy, or whatever, are not eccentric, isolated instances occurring in man's experience, but are representative of natural patterns of everyday behavior that become invisible in your world because of the official picture of behavior and reality.

The body's natural healing processes each day rid people of diseases, repair emotional or bodily illnesses — and such instances go largely unrecorded. Ruburt accepted the magic of a poem, but not the magic of health or mobility, because he was convinced that mobility stood in the way of his other abilities.

He was also convinced — as you were — that you both needed protection from the world. Many of the ideas I have given you lately were indeed in *Mass Events (as Jane remarked today),* but they have become alive now. In the same way, many other concepts and ideas already given will also assume a new significance and meaning, and add to the richness of your experience, because you will be open to them more than you were before — Ruburt in particular — to ideas having to do with reincarnation, life after death, other spheres of activity.

Ruburt instinctively likes your tree painting. It represents a certain state of consciousness — an in-between threshold dimension of awareness, in which the imagination and the senses are almost caught in the act of putting an object together, or of bringing the world into a sensed reality, brand-new, from the realm of the inner mind: a very evocative state of consciousness, and one that as I believe Ruburt mentioned, you could also use in connection with faces.

("Thanks, Seth," I said mentally to those kind words. And I've already thought of using the "technique" with faces.)

Ruburt's body is then magically and naturally repairing itself in a function just as creative, of course, as the inner work that goes on in the production of a book or a poem — a fact he is finally getting through his head. When your proofreading is over, and Ruburt's recovery even more fully demonstrable, we will return to a book session a week, and continue this series the other [weekly] session. We can also expect some improvement in vision, as that area is now being worked on.

I bid you a fond good evening — and remind me some time to add more to the material on education.

("Thank you, Seth.")

Good evening.

("Good evening."

(9:37 P.M. "I didn't think I could do it," Jane said, "but when he came around I knew I could." I told her the little session was excellent.

(I also told her something I'd thought about this afternoon, and had a bit of trouble expressing now. But these sessions, dealing with Jane's improvements, validate the Seth material as it's come to us over the years. This has a drawback, of course, in that we have no official evidence of her "symptoms" on the medical record. However, we do have the testimony of

many who know us, plus years of sessions on record, plus our own memories. [Others, I've often speculated, couldn't realize the depth of Jane's challenges.] As we talked, Jane laughed and said she picked up from Seth that "the best books are yet to come.")

NOTE: SESSION OF SEPTEMBER 10, 1980

1. Helen Bowman — Miss Bowman, my parents and I always called her — was my art teacher in the Sayre, Pennsylvania, high school from 1935 until my graduation in 1937. Through an arrangement with my mother, Stella Butts, Miss Bowman loaned me the money to attend commercial art school in New York City from 1939 to 1941. I was drafted into the Air Force in 1942, during World War II, and repaid the loan over my three years of service.

A note added 14 years after Jane/Seth delivered the magical-approach material: Miss Bowman died in 1994, at the age of 96.

SESSION ELEVEN

MULTIDIMENSIONAL SPIRITUAL DRAMAS.

SEPTEMBER 15, 1980
8:52 P.M., MONDAY

(*Today Jane has been really "out of it." She's felt a lot of muscular discomfort with her physical improvements, though, making it hard to concentrate. By 8:30, when she'd finished doing the dishes, the overall soreness had dissipated to some degree, but she appeared to be so groggy with relaxation that I hardly expected her to want to have a session. She yawned again and again. At 8:40 she surprised me by calling out from the living room — I sat reading a magazine at the kitchen table — that she'd try to have a short session. "I feel something about religion. . . ."*

("Oh, Lord," I said, joking. For I was embroiled in trying to produce a note relative to a passage of Seth's in Mass Events *about Christ's resurrection and ascension. For several reasons, interruptions among them, I'd found it difficult to get into the work, and had spent the weekend reading to remind myself of background material. I wanted the note to be coherent, without going into too much detail. Jane has also contributed an excellent paragraph of material for it. As I have before, I found the whole religious issue confusing and contradictory. And the last thing I'd expected of Jane tonight was any material on religion from Seth. Obviously, my own*

hassles about the subject were prompting her efforts, I thought.

(One of the interruptions concerned the overflow of water from a cellar bathroom. Last night I'd discovered that a portion of the cellar floor — including the old "bomb shelter" where I keep our fan mail stored — was covered by a quarter inch of water — just enough to soak into the 2 by 4's I have the cardboard boxes placed upon [to avoid water!]. If the wooden supports soak up enough water they can bleed into the very porous boxes. So I had some damp correspondence to resurrect — without too much trouble, actually. The plumber cleaned out the house's sewer line this afternoon, and I spent much time mopping up six full buckets of dirty water.

(Jane's delivery for Seth seemed to be the same as ever, except that she took longer pauses between sentences — almost as though she waited a bit each time to gather the impetus to deal with her very relaxed physical state. But the material is excellent, as usual, and I will be working with it while doing the note for Mass **Events.**)

Now: Good evening.

("Good evening, Seth.")

A few comments.

Now: Christ was not crucified — therefore he did not resurrect, coming out of the tomb, nor did he then ascend into heaven. In the terms of the biblical <u>drama</u> (underlined), however, Christ was crucified.

He arose from the tomb and ascended into heaven. The resurrection and the ascension are indeed, however, the two parts of one dramatic event. *(Pause.)* Dogmatically, arising from the dead alone was clearly not sufficient, for men were to follow where Christ led. You could not have a world in which the newly-risen dead mixed with the living. An existence in a spiritual realm had to follow such a resurrection.

(Pause.) Now in the facts of history, there was no crucifixion,

resurrection, or ascension. In the terms of history there was no biblical Christ *(pause)*, whose life followed the details given. The organization of the church is a historical fact. The power, devotion, and energy, the organizational expertise of Christianity, cannot be disputed. Nor can it be disputed that Christianity was based upon great religious and psychic vision. To some extent it involved the intuitional reorganization of subjective, and then objective, realities.

(Long pause at 9:05.) I have told you, however, that the world of events springs from the world of ideas. It seems certain that "something" happened "back then" *(as I often remark)* — and that if you could go back there, invisibly studying the century, you would discover the birth of Christianity *(also as I've remarked, although I prefer to say that "I'd like to see what did happen")*. But Christianity was not born at that time. *(Long pause.)* You might say that the labor pains *(intently)* were happening then, but the birth itself did not emerge for some time later.

Jewish shepherds represented the placenta that was meant to be discarded, for it was Jewish tradition that nourished the new religion in its early stages before its birth. Christ, as you know, was a common name, so when I say that there was a man named Christ involved in those events *(see Seth Speaks)*, I do not mean to say that he was the biblical Christ. His life was one of those lives that were finally used to compose the composite image of the biblical Christ.

The mass psyche was seeking for a change, an impetus, a flowering, a new organization. The idea of a redeemer was hardly new, but ancient in many traditions. As I stated before, that part of the world was filled with would-be messiahs, self-proclaimed prophets, and so forth, and in those terms it was only a matter of time before man's great spiritual and psychic desires illuminated and filled up that psychological landscape, filling the prepared psychological patterns with a new urgency and intent. There were many throw-away messiahs *(with gentle amusement)* — men whose circumstances, characteristics, and abilities were almost *(musically)* the ones needed — who almost *(musically)* filled the psychic bill, but who were unfitted for other reasons: They were of the wrong race, or their timing was off. Their intersection with space and time did not mesh with the requirements.

(Pause.) You must understand the long trail of psychological reality that exists before you have a physical event. You must understand man's need and capacity for fulfillment, dramatization, and psychic creativity.

There is nothing that happened in those times that is not happening now in your own: You have numberless gurus, people who seemingly perform miracles (and some do). So there were in those days some rather disconnected events that served as the focus point for great psychic activity: People wanted to believe, and their belief changed the course of history. It doesn't matter that the events never happened — the belief happened. And the belief was man's response to *(long pause)* intuitional knowledge, to inner knowing, and to spiritual comprehension.

(9:25.) These all had to flow into reality, into psychological patterns through man's own understanding. They had to flow into the events of history as he (underlined) experienced history. They had to touch the times, and they did so by transforming those times for later generations.

I want it understood *(pause)* that the accomplishment *(pause)* is breathtaking in its grandeur — more so because man formed from his psyche such a multidimensional spiritual drama that its light struck upon this or that person, this or that place, and formed a story *(pause)* more powerful than any physical event could be — hence its power *(emphatically)*.

In those terms, however, again, the gods of Olympus were as real, for all of men's riches are representations, psychic dramatizations, standing for an inner reality that cannot be literally expressed or described — but can be creatively expressed or represented.

(Long pause.) Too-literal translations of such material often lead to grief, and the creative thrust becomes lost. The great mystery, of course, and great questions, rest in the nature of that inner reality from which man weans *(repeated at my question)* his religions, and in the power of the creative abilities themselves that bring them into birth *(all quite intently)*. Such activities on a large scale are the end result of each natural person's individual relationship with nature, and with nature's source.

(Pause.) Now: Ruburt is progressing very well, and with your help, and both of you should become more and more aware of the natural persons that you are. Do you have a question?

("No, I think you've covered the material very well.")

Then I bid you a fond good evening.

("Thank you very much, Seth. Good night."

(9:38 P.M. Jane agreed with my own surprise that she not only chose to hold the session, but discussed the Christ material. She said that in spite of her being so relaxed, "There Seth was, right there. . . ." as soon as she went into trance. But now she was just as much at ease as she had been before the session. She had taken many long pauses during her delivery, a few of which I've indicated.

(Jane laughed as we talked. "You don't have to publish it, but I have the feeling that he — Seth — would have said all that earlier, a long time

ago, if I'd let him. . . ."

("Well," I said, "maybe he would have if I'd encouraged him to do so too."

(She agreed.)

SESSION TWELVE

INSERTING NEW IDEAS INTO THE WORLD.

SEPTEMBER 22, 1980
9:04 P.M., MONDAY

(*J*ane didn't hold her regularly scheduled session last Wednesday evening. She didn't particularly feel like one tonight, either, but she decided to have it rather than "sit around all night." The weather was still very humid and warm, after a 90-degree day. It's also the first evening of fall, which began at 5:09 P.M., according to TV. Jane has been doing well, though, and yesterday walked three times — the most in one day that I can remember offhand. Her general physical improvements continue.

(All week we've been doing additional medical notes for the copy-edited manuscript of Mass Events. Even today Jane talked to Tam Mossman, her editor at Prentice-Hall, about various matters involving the book. I dislike the whole situation intensely. In my frustration, I told Jane over the weekend that I intended to go back to painting, starting this morning, but it didn't work out that way. We've even considered withdrawing Mass Events from publication, although Tam reassured Jane this morning that things would work out all right. I didn't mail a long letter Jane wrote him over the weekend; she covered its points in the call this morning. Now we have an idea for our own type of "disclaimer" for the frontmatter of Mass

Events, based upon a very apt quote from Seth's material that we found late in the book. I mailed Tam a copy of it today.

(The whole affair has led to some degree of depression on my part. I told Jane that I felt the disclaimer planned for one of our books by the publisher could hardly be the end of such thinking. Overreacting, I envisioned disclaimers showing up in all of the books as they were reprinted. We discussed various scenarios over the weekend, considering the ways in which we could choose to react to the whole business.

(We hadn't asked that Seth discuss the Prentice-Hall situation this evening — but when Seth came through with a rather ironic smile. . . .)

Now: Good evening.

("Good evening, Seth.")

I have a few pithy comments.

I would like to give you some insight as to why Prentice-Hall is our publisher to begin with. Maybe we can, in that way, clear up a matter that often seems to contain some mystery *(amused.*

("That certainly would be nice.")

Once said, the explanation will certainly seem obvious. *(Pause.)* Prentice-Hall, in capsule form, so to speak, is a representative of the most diverse kinds of thought currently held in your country — that is, under it's overall auspices you have the most conventional establishment-oriented textbooks, devoted to continuing traditional ideas. You have, there, a concentration upon education as it is understood at that level.

Under Prentice's auspices, however, you also have Parker Books — books that are devoted to quite anti-establishment ideas and concepts — to all brands of psychic, scientific, or religious eccentricities, given to matters that contradict the establishment and challenge it at every point. And there, too, you have a concentration upon education, in that the books are written to instruct.

Our books do not appear under the Parker heading. *(Long pause.)* They are in their way bridges between the two opposing ways of thought. They are too anti-establishment to be college textbooks, but in their way far too reasonable to be considered eccentricities — in the same fashion, now, that the Parker books are.

Our books are in the regular trade department. This poses some problems for the legal department, which is given to the most literal translation of reality as interpreted through law. You have almost what you could call a schizophrenic relationship, existing, say, between Parker Books and Prentice's trade-book division. The textbook division represents the workings of the intellect in the usual terms of rational thought, and in those books the qualities of the imagination, of the psyche, of poetry, of creativity, are quite lacking. Such qualities are indeed considered threats, for they do not accept easy answers, and are not content with the status quo.

Many of the Parker books on the other hand emphasize creativity, the intuitions, the use of the imagination, but are relatively innocent of any clear reasoning, logic, or any feeling for tradition at all. I am simplifying here to some extent to make my point. Prentice is always, then, to some extent in a state of creative tension, as the seemingly opposed, seemingly contradictory elements are each expressed through these two divisions.

(Long pause.) Because of those divisions, however, there is indeed a great publishing leeway possible of books that otherwise could not mingle.

(9:23.) Give us a moment . . . Prentice does more than it knows it does. As a corporate entity, it also has a conscious and unconscious intent, as do all organizations, because they must mirror the people who belong to them. In its way Prentice is an

educational institution. It tries to fly ahead with avant garde ideas, while at the same time protecting its flank of college textbooks. *(With amusement:)* It does not know if our work is fact or fiction, in the deepest of terms. It knows the work is not forged. It knows that I appear in sessions, for example, but it does not know whether or not my ideas correspond with a greater reality, or whether they are the result of an extraordinary psychological creativity.

Those same characteristics I have mentioned as applying to Prentice apply in their way to Tam, of course. He can indeed express great enthusiasm over work that is highly intuitional, while on the other hand he has a great respect, in his own way, for established learning and education.

Now with the various people at Prentice, you will have such tendencies often appearing separately, so that one person will be highly conventional and dislike changes, while another might be responsive to work that was emotionally exciting, avant garde. The publishing house — that publishing house — represents in capsule form the extremes of thought of your time, from the most conventional to the most bizarre. It therefore represents the public's ideas in their great variety.

The legal department knows how to deal with the Parker books. *(Tam told Jane it's putting disclaimers in all Parker books.)* It knows how to deal with fiction. It knows how to deal with conventional textbooks — but in a fashion our books combine all of those elements, and transcend them. If Prentice were as conventional at heart as its legal department, it would not publish books at all, except perhaps for the textbooks.

Our books are attempting to insert new ideas into the world as it now is, by combining the powers of the intellect and the powers of the intuitions — in other words, by closing the two ends of Prentice's extremes.

(Long pause.) Now: We have been dealing with the magical approach, and let me gently remind the two of you that I said that you must be willing to change all the way from the old system of orientation to the new, if you want the new approach to work fully for you in your lives. That will, as it happens, include your approach to Prentice, of course.

Now: As I said before, also, when faced with the difficulty, the conventional, rational approach tells you to look at the problem, examine it thoroughly, project it into the future, and imagine its dire consequences — and so, faced with the idea of a disclaimer *(for Mass Events)*, that is what you did to some extent, the two of you. You saw the disclaimer as fact, imagined it in your minds on the pages of our books, projected all of that onto future books, and for fine good measure you both imagined this famous disclaimer published in editions of all the books as well.

That is an excellent example of what not to do.

(9:42.) Indeed, you both began to pull out of that yourselves. You did at least question the approach. In the meantime, of course, your nervous systems reacted to the implied threat against your work, a threat that now existed in the past, present, and future.

(Intently in a fast delivery:) You are protected. Your work is protected. When you realize that, you act out of confidence. You did indeed catch yourselves. Ruburt mentioned those concerns, but not with the same kind of feelings that he would have, say, [last] Saturday — and when you realize that you are protected, your own intellects can be reassured enough through experience so that they do not feel the need to solve problems with the rational

approach in instances where that approach is not <u>feasible</u>.

<u>In the deepest of terms it was not reasonable</u> (underlined) to nearly assume that a disclaimer, if used, would therefore be retroactively and then continuously used. It was not a conclusion based upon fact, but a conclusion based upon a reason that applied to one probability only, one series of probable acts — or based upon the probable act of a disclaimer being used to begin with.[1] So again, what we are dealing with is an overall lesson in <u>the way in which the reasoning mind has been taught to react.</u> These are really instances where the intellect has been trained to use only a portion of its abilities, to zoom in on the most pessimistic of any given series of probable actions — <u>and then treat those as if they were facts.</u>

(Louder:) And let me add, I covered our flank in the book —

("You certainly did." Seth's amused reference was to manuscript page 457 in Mass Events. *Jane and I decided to use his passage, with a note, in the frontmatter of the book, for he stressed that until they're mentally clear about their beliefs people should continue to see doctors.)*

— but do not forget that you in your ways, and that corporate entity, do indeed share an educational intent.

I will, of course, have more to say that will hopefully allow you to use your intellects in a clear fashion, to better your performances. You are quite right, again, to say that "There are elements in this situation — or in any given situation — impossible for my intellect to know," so the intellect can take that fact into consideration. Otherwise, you expect it to make deductions while denying it the comfort it should have, of knowing that its deductions need not be made on its own knowledge alone, but on the intuition's vast magical bank of information — from which, in larger terms, <u>all</u> of the intellect's information must spring. So I think you are both finally trying to use a new approach in that direction.

(9:59.) Now: Ruburt's condition is coming along very well. He is feeling more active, and he will. And he should read the last group of sessions frequently. *(Pause.)* Do you have a question?

("I guess not.")

Do your painting of your light experience[2] — and of course continue with your [other] painting.

Ruburt is anxious that Prentice present our books in the best light in the world. They also have their own paranoid tendencies, and overworked intellects to contend with. The magical approach will get you through, if you use it.

My heartiest regards, and a fond good evening *(with a pleased, quiet intensity.*

("Thank you very much, Seth. Good night.")

(10:04 P.M. For someone who hadn't felt like having a session, Jane did very well.)

NOTES: SESSION OF SEPTEMBER 22, 1980

1. Seth was right. It never happened: For all of our worries, those in charge at Prentice-Hall did not decide to use disclaimers of responsibility in any of Jane's other books.

2. From my dream notebook:
"Vision, 11:45 P.M., Sunday, September 21, 1980:
"I lay on our bed, fully clothed, while waiting for Jane to finish in the bathroom. As usual, the little light on her bureau to my right was on. I lay flat on my back, with my head turned a little toward the dim light. I was quite sleepy, and fell into a state between waking and sleeping. Then I became aware that once again I was perceiving "the light of the universe," as Seth calls it. This experience was milder than my three previous ones, but was still most intriguing.

"I don't want to complicate it by speculating about being in an out-of-body state while having it. I realized that while lying on my back with my head turned a bit to the right, I was definitely looking to my *left*, at the top of a plain, solid wooden door to a room — and that my viewpoint was up, just above the top of the door in its frame, which was close to a low ceiling. The door was dark on my side, and was open toward me perhaps three inches at the most.

"Now *behind* the door was a brilliant pulsing light — but I could see only the small portion of it at the top of the nearly-shut door. My reactions during the experience were quite objective this time. I knew what I was creating. I had none of the thrilling sensations, for example, that can sweep over me at such times.

"As I came out of the experience a few moments later I resolved to paint a small oil of it, as I've done following my three previous perceptions of the light of the universe this year — on February 9 and 10, and on June 16. And it's obvious that in tonight's little adventure I had once again cleverly protected myself from confronting the full creative blast of the light of the universe by allowing myself just a peek at it, and a careful one at that, at the top of the door. Seth has told me that as a physical creature I'd be overwhelmed if ever I came even close to facing that awesome conscious and creative power."

(See my painting at the end of this session.)

Robert F. Butts (1919–): *Beyond the Door.* 1980. Oil on panel, 13 x 10⅞ in.

It was impossible for me to even approach with mundane physical paint the pulsating brilliance of that tiny bit of the "light of the universe" that I allowed myself to experience at the top of the nearly-closed door.

SESSION THIRTEEN

SEPTEMBER 24, 1980
9:24 P.M., WEDNESDAY

(*J ane hasn't felt her best today: She's had a lot of soreness because of muscular changes taking place. First she decided to see if she could have a session, then at 9:10 she decided against it. But when I said I'd return to typing Monday night's session, in a rather humorous turnabout she decided to hold a session tonight after all. "If he comes through he'll be doing good," she said. "I don't feel him around." As I wrote these notes at 9:20, however, she did begin to feel Seth's presence. "You're not deserted after all," I said.*

(Just before we sat for the session Jane finished reading my account of my "light of the universe" experience of last Sunday evening, September 21, and my account of the experience involving . . . clairvoyance . . . precognition . . . that I'd had at naptime today, involving my idea for a novel and an article in tonight's Star-Gazette, *Elmira's daily newspaper. I describe both of these events in my dream notebook.*

("I wish there were words to use besides clairvoyance or precognition," I said, since I was somewhat reluctant to attach them to the newspaper experience. That is, at the time I hadn't had any feeling that those qualities

or terms might apply to what I'd sensed — nor do I now. Perhaps I was merely afraid the experience wasn't clairvoyant, I said, yet I felt our vocabulary was limited in some indefinable way in such cases. A copy of my newspaper experience is attached to this session.[1]

(I must say that I hadn't expected Seth to discuss the event this evening, nor had I asked that he do so. Also, for someone who wasn't sure they wanted to hold a session to begin with, Jane's delivery was excellent — usually fast and quite emphatic throughout.)

Now: Comments.

("Good evening.")

If you had first read the article of which you have been speaking, and then in a semi-dozing state created your idea of a novel, replete with the characterization of the mother, then you would say that cause and effect were involved.

Science might admit that the novel idea itself was highly creative, an example of the mind at play as it used experience as a creative raw product — but of course you had your experience <u>before</u> you read the article. And when that kind of thing happens science then proclaims that the two events are not connected to each other at all, but are instead the result of coincidental patterns.

In your terms, whether a minute or 10 minutes, or an hour or two hours were involved, you reacted ahead of time to a headline that you had not as yet physically encountered. You reacted creatively, using the precognitive story as a basis for a fictional endeavor. You turned it to art's purposes.

(9:31.) Give us a moment . . . As you lay there you were aware of the fact just beneath consciousness — usual consciousness — that you had not brought in the paper before your nap, as is your habit, and almost at a dream level you idly wondered what stories

· 107 ·

it might contain. Your inclusion of the hospital mixup in the tale was, as, you suspected, connected with the medical ideas you have been dealing with of late *(in extra notes for Mass Events, and the book by the physician)* — and here was an excellent fictional idea, you see, that could, among other things, bring those ideas into prominence.

The idea, then, of the novel came from past and future events, though you were to catch up with those future events very quickly. Your mind intuitively organized all of that material, and put it together in a completely new fashion. Sometimes when such events occur, the precognitive trigger is not even recognized when it is encountered physically, because it happens too far ahead of time. *(To me:)* You organize mental and physical events in a creative manner. In this case a novel was involved because the concept, while strongly involving images, carried a time span that would make narrative necessary.

You used the magical approach. You caught yourself in the act of acting naturally, of demonstrating abilities that your society to a large degree does not admit. That same kind of lightning-swift organization goes on within the body itself constantly, as it deals with probable scenarios to which you may or may not end up reacting to.

The events themselves discussed in the newspaper article point up the same kind of magical affiliations. The c-e-l-l-s *(spelled)* of the young men in question were always in communication, and all of those elements needed to bring about such a reunion took place at that magical level of activity. Consciously, intellectually, the boys had no idea they were triplets. You live personally in a world of lush creative ideas. Your intellect is aware of that. *(Pause.)* It is used to working creatively. The focused intellect can indeed activate the intuitive abilities — and the <u>healing</u> abilities. You get what you concentrate upon.

(9:45.) The intellect is a vital organizer even if it is not aware of the magical levels of activity from which often its best ideas emerge.

This will be a very brief session. When you look at world events, however, the present world situation for example *(the war between Iraq and Iran, which began a few days ago)*, try to enlarge the scope of your intellectual reach, so that you consider world events as living multidimensional "novels" being formed in the present in <u>response to</u> both future and past triggers. The impact of the future on the past, in your terms — or rather, the implications of the future on the present — are highly important, and such precognitive reactions are as vital, numerous, and real as you ordinarily think that the reactions to past events are *(intently)*.

This puts present world events in an entirely different perspective. Men act, then, in relationship to events that have, historically speaking, not yet occurred — but those events happening, say, in the future, <u>in certain terms</u> cast their shadows back into the present, or <u>illuminate</u> the past according to the events' characteristics. There is always more going on than ordinary sense data show.

In your comparatively simple experience, you can see, however, the implications of such activities. Men may react to future events by unconsciously translating them into art, or motion pictures. They may react by unconsciously taking certain steps of a political nature that seem at the time either unreasonable, or even incomprehensible — steps whose <u>logic</u> appears only in hindsight.

The same occurs, of course, in all areas of human behavior, as well as in the behavior of animals and even of plants. This future shadowing the present, or future illuminating the present, represents a vital element in the formation of events as they are perceived in time. In a fashion the triplets were reacting in their past to a future event that has now caught up with them, so that each of their actions in any moment of that past happened as a result of a tension — a creative tension — between the event of their original separation and the event of their future reunion.

I do not mean that the reunion was inevitable or predestined, but the vigor of that probability, you might say, magnified the original tension. I want Ruburt to apply all of this to his own situation, both in terms of creative endeavors and his physical situation, so that he begins to understand that he can start to react in the present to a future recovery.

(Long pause at 10:01.) He can see how important periods of letting go are. Your experience happened when you were nearly asleep, but merely relaxed, not worrying, with your intellect in a kind of free flow. You were not hampering it. It was momentarily free of limiting beliefs, and it naturally used — and chose to use — the magical approach to answer what was a very simple, now-forgotten intellectual question: What might be in today's newspaper?

The usual answer, or the usual method of obtaining an answer, was at the time inconvenient: You were not about to get up, go outside and get the paper, so on its own the intellect pressed the magical-approach button, you might say, getting the information the quickest and easiest way possible.

It did not give you the bare headline, however — even though that and the story were perceived far too quickly for you to follow. What you were aware of were your own creative reveries in response to that information.

Now left alone, the intellect will often solve problems in just such a fashion, <u>when</u> it is allowed to, <u>when</u> you forget what is supposed to be possible and what is not, <u>when</u> you forget that your mind is supposed to be pedestrian and parochial.

(Pause.) End of session —

(I smiled at Seth as "he" leaned toward me. "I thought so. It's been very interesting.")

— and a fond good evening.

("Thank you. The same to you. Good night."

(10:09 P.M. "Brilliant, hon," I said to Jane as she quickly came out of her trance state. She was pleased. For someone who hadn't known whether they wanted a session, she'd done very well, with her delivery being often fast and emphatic. I told her that it looked as though Seth used my newspaper incident to actually summarize in capsule form much of the material he's been giving us in this latest group of private sessions. "You couldn't ask for a better demonstration of the whole thing," I said.

(I intend to copy a page or two of the session to insert in my notebook containing suggestions of notes for Dreams, *Seth's latest book. I mean the material about time. I also thought we should somehow keep the session in mind, and not let it get lost in the files as the years pass — one of the reasons I want to use part of it in* Dreams. *Since it's private, it might not be published any time soon otherwise.*

(A note: the way things "work" . . . On Thursday morning — the day after this session was held — Jane and I saw the three young men referred to in the newspaper article on a well-known variety show. Very interesting. One of them said he'd had "a dream" about having brothers. The others weren't as definite, but at least indicated they hadn't felt alone. The TV host never referred to the fact that the three youths were actually members of quadruplets — that a fourth brother had died at birth, according to the news article. Neither did the brothers. I also mentioned to Jane the similarity in the adoptive last names of two of the brothers: Kellman and Gelland.)

1. Experience, 4:00 P.M., Wednesday, September 24, 1980.

I lay down for a nap in the bedroom after Jane got up from her own. I had the following ideas as I lay in that state between waking and sleeping. I found myself musing about what I thought was a great idea for a novel. I tried to describe it to Jane as we ate supper and watched the news on TV.

I thought of myself as a woman at the mall in Big Flats, near Elmira. As I went through a double revolving door I caught a glimpse of a young man, say in his mid-twenties, who was an exact duplicate of my own son, who I knew was not in the mall, but was away on business of some kind. The shock of seeing my son's double was so great that instead of chasing him to question him, I had to sit down on a bench to recover. By then the young man was gone. I envisioned myself returning to the mall again and again to see if I could see the person — and finally I did. Either I followed him to his car, then talked to him, or followed him to where he lived with his parents — but he bore an uncanny resemblance to my own son.

I do not know how or when the two look-a-like young men met — but in my reverie I thought of the mother in question tracing back connections all the way to her son's birth at the Elmira hospital. I envisioned the delivery rooms there, and the room where visitors see their babies (I've never seen those rooms in "real" life).

The story unfolds when the mother uncovers evidence of a mixup in the baby complex at the hospital: She had been given only one of her children, or some such affair; either that, or she had managed to adopt a baby from there. Either way, she finds out through much detective work that a whole series of mixups had occurred in the hospital that day — that in the Elmira area there are several sets of parents who have been raising the wrong children all these years. There had been mixups in the hospital because of new help, etc. I thought it would make a great novel as all of the entangled threads were unwound, and considering the emotional tangles that had been built up over the years as parents raised children they thought were theirs.

I think that the idea of mixups in the hospital came from a book Jane and I have been reading the past week, written by a doctor who warns against medicine, delivery rooms, the whole bit, in the establishment practice of medicine. He wrote that such baby mixups are far from rare. Then as we sat on the couch, I remembered that for the first time in literally months I'd forgotten to bring in the evening paper, so we could look at it while we ate and watched TV. I almost invariably bring in the paper before I lay down for a nap before supper, so Jane can read it while I sleep.

On the front page of the paper was a rather long story, with photographs, telling how triplets were united by "chance" last weekend in New York City — a case we hadn't heard of in the media before now. I'd forgotten to describe my idea for a novel to Jane, but the article immediately reminded me to do so. There were similarities in the story that reminded me of my own experience. The first two of the brothers were reunited through a friend (instead of a mother, say) who noticed the resemblance between them. Turns out the three were given up for adoption at birth, and although they knew they were adopted, they didn't know they belonged to what actually had been a quadruplet group. (A fourth brother had died at birth.) Their unknowing would match my own dreamlike idea of the two young men living in the Elmira area but not knowing of each other. Even the ages of the triplets — 19 years — places them fairly close to my son's age of 25 in my reverie, rather than, for example, brothers in their 40s.

I was quite struck by the similarities between the news story and my own experience. Jane thinks that because I forgot to bring in the paper before I lay down, I may have tuned into it, out there in the box beside the mailbox. I didn't have any strong feeling that I had, however, but get a few thrills as I finish this account.

I should add that I lay down at about 4:20. On weekdays the motor carrier usually leaves the paper in its box around 3:15–3:30, so the paper was "in position" for me to zoom in on it. In fact, we can see our box on the road from our bedroom windows, looking slightly north. I pull the shades before lying down. I don't remember if I happened to glance at the box today while lowering them. The box is perhaps 45–50 feet from the bedroom windows, and its backend is toward our house. I can tell if the paper has come, though, by looking across the road into our neighbor's box. On weekends, when the paper is delivered in the morning, and is sometimes late, I often check the neighbor's box.

SESSION FOURTEEN

THE SELF. RELAXATION AND EFFORTLESSNESS.

SEPTEMBER 29, 1980
9:18 P.M., MONDAY

(I have but a few sessions left to check on the copy-edited manuscript for
Mass Events. *Then I can start correlating it with the first carbon
[which we keep], before mailing the manuscript back to Prentice-Hall,
probably late this week, for printing. The book is scheduled to be in the
stores in May 1981.*

*(Jane continues her improvements, although she's been having periods
of worry and doubt. Now she waited impatiently for Seth to come through:
At first I'd thought she would pass up the session. Finally she felt her boy
around. "I'm glad," I joked. "I was afraid he might only get as far as
Coleman Avenue — a block away — or someplace like that. I didn't want
to sit around waiting, and wasting my time. . . . .")*

Now —

("Good evening.")

It is not true, of course, that before the time of modern psychology man had a concept of himself that dealt with conscious
exterior aspects only, although it has been written that until that
time man thought of himself as a kind of flat-surfaced self —

minus, for example, subconscious or unconscious complexity.

Instead, previous to psychology's entrance, before psychology mapped the acceptable or forbidden, the dangerous or safe compartments of the self, man used the word "soul" to include his own entire complexity. That word was large enough to contain man's experience. It was large enough to provide room for conventional and unconventional, bizarre and ordinary states of mind and experience. It was roomy enough to hold images of reality that were physically perceived or psychologically perceived.

Now the church finally placed all of the condemnation of its religious laws against certain psychological and mystical experiences — not because it did not consider them realities, of course, but precisely because it recognized too well the disruptive influence that, say, revelationary experience could have upon a world order that was based upon a uniform dogma.

"Witches" were not considered insane, for example, or deranged, for their psychological beliefs fit in only too well with those of the general populace. They were considered evil instead. *(Pause.)* The vast range of psychological expression, however, had some kind of framework to contain it. *(Pause.)* The saint and the sinner *(pause)* each had access to great depths of possible heroism or despair. Psychological reality, for all of the religious *(pause)* dangers placed upon it, was anything but a flat-surfaced experience. It was in fact because the church so believed in the great range of psychological activity possible that it was so dogmatic and tireless in trying to maintain order.

(Long pause at 9:33.) Unfortunately, with the development of the scientific era, a development occurred that need not have happened. As I have mentioned before, science's determination to be objective almost immediately brought about a certain artificial

shrinking of psychological reality. What could not be proven in the laboratory was presumed not to exist at all.

Anyone who experienced "something that could not exist" was therefore to some extent or another deluded or deranged. There is no doubt that the <u>accepted</u> dimensions of psychological reality began to shrink precisely at the time that modern psychology began. *(Long pause.)* Modern psychology was an attempt to make man <u>conform</u> to the new scientific world view.

It was an attempt to fit man within the picture of evolution, and to manufacture a creature whose very existence was somehow pitted against itself. Evolutionary man, with Darwinian roots, could not be a creature with a soul. It had to have hidden in its psychological roots the bloody remnants of the struggle for survival that now cast it in its uneasy role. *(Pause.)* There is no doubt that the church cast the soul in a position of <u>stress</u>, caught as it was between its heavenly source and original sin — but there was a sense of psychological mobility involved, one that saw continued existence after death.

The new psychology shut off mobility after death, while giving each individual an unsavory primitive past heritage — a heritage genetically carried, that led finally only to the grave. *(Long pause.)* Psychological activity was scaled down in between life and death, then, even while the possibility of any after-death experience was considered the most unreasonable and unintellectual of speculations.

(Long pause at 9:43.) Any man might rise in your democracy from a poor peasant's son to be the President. Outcasts might become the socially prominent. The unlettered might become highly educated. The idea of achieving greatness, however, was considered highly suspect. The self was kept in bounds. Great passion, or desire or intent — or genius — did not fit the picture.

(Long pause.) Now some peoples would not fit into that mold. They would take what they could from your technology, but in conscious and spontaneous ways they retaliated — and still do — by exaggerating all of those human tendencies that your society has held down so well. If you can have reason without faith, then indeed, for example, you will see that there can be faith without reason. When human experience becomes shrunken in such a fashion — compressed — then in a fashion it also explodes at both ends, you might say.

You have atrocious acts committed, along with great heroisms, but each are explosive, representing sudden releases of withheld energies that have in other ways been forbidden, and so man's mass psyche expresses itself sometimes like explosive fireworks, simply because the release of pressure is necessary.

Even your poor misguided moral/religious organization is saying in its fashion to the scientifically-oriented society: "How is faith not real, then? We'll change your laws with it. We'll turn it into power — political power. What will you say then? We have been laughed at for so long. We will see who laughs now."

Fanaticism abounds, of course, because the human tendencies and experiences that have been denied by the mainline society erupt with explosive force, where the tendencies themselves must be accepted as characteristics of human experience. Iran is an example for the world, in explosive capsule form, complete with historical background and a modern political one. Modern psychology does not have a concept of the self to begin to explain such realities.

Now, in the world you *(to me)* early formed your own beliefs and strategies. In midlife you were presented with our sessions — or [the two of] you presented yourselves with them, if you prefer.

You recognized the overall <u>vitality</u> of our material *(long pause)* — but again, you did not realize that it meant a complete reorientation of your attitudes. You did not realize that you were being presented, not merely with an alternate view of reality, but with the closest approximation you could get of what reality was, and how it worked, and what it meant.

(10:07.) I have <u>been very gentle</u> in my treatment of your mores and institutions — for I do not want you to be against your world, but for a more fulfilling one. Toward the end of our present book *(Dreams)*, we will be discussing how our ideas can be applied by the individual in terms of value fulfillment, so that individuals can begin to reclaim those dimensions of experience that are indeed your rightful heritage.

Now: For Ruburt, I want him to remember the <u>idea</u> of effortlessness, because with the best of intentions he has been trying too hard. *(Pause.)* I want him to remember that relaxation is one of creativity's greatest <u>champions</u> — not its enemy. He is naturally gifted with the quickness of body and mind. Remind him that it is safe to express his <u>natural</u> (underlined) rhythms, to remember the natural person. Your most vital inspirations are effortlessly yours. I want you to see how many of your beliefs are the result of the old framework, for in that way you will find yourselves releasing yourselves more and more, so that your own strengths come to your support.

End of session, and a fond good evening.

("Thank you, Seth.")

(10:14 P.M. Jane had no idea of most of the material in the session — that is, she hadn't known Seth was going to deliver it. Now, however, she remembered that just before the session she'd picked up the idea that Seth would mention effortlessness in connection with her own situation.)

SESSION FIFTEEN

THE NATURAL PERSON AND THE NATURAL USE OF TIME.

OCTOBER 1, 1980
9:31 P.M., WEDNESDAY

(D)*uring her mid-morning exercise-and-rest break today, I asked Jane if she had any idea why Seth had come through with the material he'd given us in last Monday evening's session. At first she said no, rather matter-of-factly. Then: "Well, I don't tell you everything, but for some time now I've known Seth gives what I call 'fill-in' sessions, or 'floating material' — stuff he could give any time. It isn't private, really, or book work either. They're like 'maintenance sessions.' It's good material, all right, but. . . ."*

("So after all these years I find that out," I answered. "What else haven't you told me? How come the big secret?"

("You never asked me," she said, which had a familiar ring. [Checking later, I found that she'd given me the same answer about certain Seth material in Mass Events.]

("Well, I can't ask you about something I don't suspect," I said. I asked her to write a short account of what she'd just told me, and she produced it while sitting in bed, after she'd done her exercises:

("October 1/80. There are certain sessions I've labelled 'fill-in' sessions

in my mind for some time now, or thought of them as covering 'floating material.' They aren't book sessions or specifically personal ones. They keep the sessions going over periods of time. Like maintenance sessions, but usually by discussing past material — connecting it with the present ['connective sessions' is more like it] — while not necessarily adding new thrust. And not specifically *given to one subject.*

("Originally the Christ sessions started that way.

("I think such connective sessions happen between book sessions, for a change of pace — where material doesn't have to fit a more concentrated overall book focus. 11:15 A.M."

(Jane has grown increasingly restless over the breaks in her activities that are caused by the rest periods she's taking several times daily. At the same time her back, for example, has improved considerably. She was angry as we sat for the session. "I'm so mad I can't talk about it," she said — while talking about it for some 20 minutes. I told her I knew she didn't want to take the rest periods, and that I had little to offer as an alternative, beyond her simply cutting down on them. I figured she'd be altering her schedule. "Boy, Seth, you'd better bail me out," she said vehemently. "I can't have a session on it because I'm too involved — you have to calm down before you can do that. . . ."

(I did say that her walking was the key to recovery: The more she walked, the less the pressure in any consistent way on other parts of her anatomy. Yet I couldn't equate the few moments she spent walking with the half-hour rest periods, either.

(In spite of her protestations, however, Jane felt Seth near as we talked — then when he came through he did *discuss the subjects we were concerned about at the moment.)*

Now: Comments.

(I nodded.)

Our friend is now feeling somewhat more ambitious of late. A few weeks ago, he could hardly wait to lie down at the appointed times, like it otherwise or no, simply because he was so uncomfortable.

Now, things have changed somewhat. The sharp discomfort has gone. A few weeks ago he barely considered taking two steps in the kitchen, much less walking twice the length of the living room, or considering walking after dinner.

The fact that he is now thinking of walking after dinner is an obvious advance. His irritability is somewhat natural — but also based on the idea, still, that when he is laying down that is dead time *(with amusement)*, or useless time, enforced inactivity. It would help, of course, if he reminded himself that his creative mind is at work whether or not he is aware of it, and regardless of what he is doing, and that such periods have the potential, at least, of accelerating creativity, if he allows his intellect to go into a kind of free drive at such times. You might have him become more aware of when he actually becomes tired, or uncomfortable, so that he does lay down then.

The walking after dinner would be excellent, of course — the idea being, however, that if he became uncomfortable from sitting that he lie on the bed, perhaps before watching television for the evening.

One important point, again, is to remember that in any given day his mood is often excellent for many periods of time. He should concentrate his attention upon those periods, rather than concentrating upon the periods when he is blue or upset, and berating himself for those reactions.

In that way, the good moods become longer. They increase. They (underlined) become significant. In such ways he will discover what promotes these good moods. Later, I will have some things to say about what I will call "the daily hypothesis," for each person has such a daily hypothesis — one that might be quite different for, say, Friday than it is for Monday. You build your daily experience partially by such working hypotheses.

(9:44 in a fast delivery.) Give us a moment. . . .*(Long pause.)* To some extent Ruburt's dissatisfaction with laying down after dinner also means that he is learning more about his own natural rhythms, for he does feel accelerated at that time, and by the evening, as you do. This is because many of the beliefs that you have individually and jointly are somewhat relieved in the evening, in that they so often apply to the day's activities, when the rest of the world seems to be engaged in the nine-to-five assembly-line world experience.

You do not project as many negative ideas upon the evening hours, and the same applies to most people to varying degrees. That is at least one of the reasons why these sessions have been held in the evening, where it was at least not as likely that you would try to invest them with the workaday kind of world values.

That is also why it is easier, generally speaking, for Ruburt to receive such information in the evening, because you are jointly free of limitations that might hamper you at other times of the day — not simply that visitors might arrive more usually then, but because you yourselves are less visited by preconceptions of what you are supposed to do in any given hour of the day.

The natural, magical flows of your own rhythms are more often broken up in the daytime. This applies to other people as well, because of your ideas of what you should be doing at any given time, or what is socially respectable, proper, upright, even moral *(wryly)* in limited terms.

(Long pause.) You have settled upon a system that seems to be

naturally based, the exclusive results of your historic past, one in which your main activities are daytime ones. It seems only natural that early man, for example, carried on all of his main activities in the day, hiding after dark. *(Pause.)* As a matter of fact, however, early man was a natural night dweller, and early developed the uses of fire for illumination, carrying on many activities after dark, when many natural predators slept. He also hunted very well in the dark, cleverly using all of his senses with high accuracy — the result of learning processes that are now quite lost.

(10:00.) In any case, man was not by any means exclusively a daytime creature, and fires within caves extended activities far into the night. It was agriculture that turned him more into a day-time rhythm, and for some time many beliefs lingered that result-ed from earlier nighttime agricultural practices.

Many people's natural rhythms, then, still do incline in those directions, and they are always kept operable as alternate rhythms for the species as a whole.

Ruburt has some inclinations in that direction, as do many creative people, but these rhythms are often nearly completely overlaid by culturally-learned ones. Cultures that were night-ori-ented *(pause)* appreciated the night in a different fashion, of course, and actually utilized their consciousnesses *(pause)* in ways that are almost nearly forgotten. I believe there are ancient fairy tales and myths still surviving that speak of these underworlds, or worlds of darkness — but they do not mean worlds of death, as is usually interpreted.

In a fashion, the intellect goes hand-in-hand with the imagina-tion under such conditions. It is not that man stressed physical data less, but that he put it together differently — that in the darkness he relied upon his inner and outer senses in a more unified fashion. The nightly portions of your personalities have become strangers to you — for as you identify with what you think of as your rational intellect, then you identify it further with the daytime hours, with the objective world that becomes visible in the morning, with the clearcut physical objects that are then before your view.

(10:10.) In those times, however, man identified more with his intuitive self, and with his imagination, and these to some extent more than now, directed the uses to which he put his intellect.

This meant, of course, a language (pause) that was in its way more precise than your own, for concepts were routinely expressed that described the vast complexity of subjective as well as objective events. (Pause.) There were myriad relationships, for example, impossible now to describe, between a person and his or her dream selves, and between the dream selves of all the members of the tribe. Particularly in warmer climates, man was naturally nocturnal, and did a good deal of his sleeping and dreaming in the daytime.

You must remember, of course, that the use of clocks is a fairly recent phenomenon. (Pause.) Men thought in terms of rhythms of the time, or of flowing time, not of time in sections that were arbitrary. So as far as creaturehood is concerned, you have adapted to a time environment that you yourselves have formed. Creative people, again, are often aware of those connections, at least at certain levels, and Ruburt in particular has always felt that way to some extent. You have largely buried your own natural feelings in that direction.

It is up to you whether you want to call this a fill-in session or not —

("I was just going to ask you about that.")

Those are Ruburt's designations, not mine. Do you have a question?

(*"No, that was it, about the fill-in session."*)

The sessions from the beginning were based upon the natural flow of Ruburt's energy, taking advantage of it in such a fashion.

End of session — but those rhythms are also more natural to you than you have suspected. You often have freedoms, then, that you do not use — a 24-hour period that you use quite arbitrarily, one that is already sectioned for you by society — but only if you allow it to be. It can be used in any fashion that you wish.

(*"Well" I said, somewhat defensively, "I've always enjoyed having the sessions at night, working after supper, and so forth."*)

You barely touch the surfaces of the kind of freedom that I am speaking of, though you certainly do far better than most.

A fond good evening —

(*"Thank you very much."*)

— and this is partially in response to your comments about the evening hours.

(*10:25 P.M. Jane had no idea ". . . what he was going to say, or anything." And note that she did manage to have a session tonight about her own challenges, even though she was quite upset because of them at the same time. Her delivery had, in fact, often been fast and forceful.*

(*After the session I reminded Jane that she'd just given a terrific session — something that no one else could do — but that she didn't give herself much credit for it. My remarks came about because as she sat on the couch after the session she said that she hadn't done anything today ". . . but sleep and lay around. . . ."*)

SESSION SIXTEEN

OCTOBER 6, 1980
9:14 P.M., MONDAY

(The following private material is from the regular 920th session. Seth often did this — whether we asked him to or not — closing out book and/or general sessions with comments of varying length for Jane and me.

(10:38.) A note: Ruburt's body is continuing to respond. The legs and arms are lengthening, and becoming stronger. He should be feeling increased quickness of motion in some respects soon. He is doing well, concentrating upon the good moods, which have increased as a result. And I bid you both a fond good evening.

("Thank you, Seth."

(Seth nodded and closed Jane's eyes.

("Good night."

(10:40 P.M.)

SESSION SEVENTEEN

JANE'S SKILL AS ANCIENT AS MAN IS.
THE SPECIES' MULTITUDINOUS ABILITIES.

OCTOBER 15, 1980
8:55 P.M., WEDNESDAY

(At lunch today I read the latest group of poems Jane has prepared for her book of poetry for Prentice-Hall.[1]

(The second game of the World Series started at 8:30 — I think — tonight, although I hardly glanced at it on television as we made ready for the session; the set went off after the first [scoreless] inning anyhow. I had a letter half done for Jeanne Miles, my well-known artist friend who lives in New York City. Mitzi was chasing one of her paperfoil toys down the cellar stairs. . . .

(I'd just finished typing the last few pages for Monday night's session, and I asked Jane what she thought of my final note: I'd speculated about any reincarnational connections that might tie her abilities to speak for Seth, without help of any modern kind, to the abilities ancient man had displayed, when, according to Seth, he'd been able to carry all of his history with him mentally. As ancient man had lived without the news media we're so used to, so does Jane speak for Seth without all of that modern help. I hadn't expected Seth to go into related material this evening.)

Good evening.

("Good evening, Seth.")

Now: Ruburt's skill is as ancient as man is, and indeed all of your arts, sciences, and cultural achievements are the offshoots of *(pause)* spontaneous mental and biological processes.

(Pause, one of many.) I choose my words quite carefully at times, because I realize the various interpretations that can be placed upon them. Perhaps the following explanation will express more clearly what I mean.

In the first place, as often mentioned lately, the reasoning mind is spontaneously fired. The species contains within itself all of the necessary spontaneous attributes that are necessary to form a civilization, for example. *(Pause.)* All of your reasoned activities — your governments, societies, arts, religions and sciences — are the physical realization, of course, of inner capacities, capacities that are inherent in man's structure. Take your theaters' moving picture dramas. These are the materialization in your time of man's natural acting ability — a characteristic highly important in the behavior of the species.

Early man, for example, spontaneously played at acting out the part of other animals. He took the part of a tree, a brook, a rock. Acting became a teaching method — a way of passing on information. *(Long pause.)* Man always possessed all of the knowledge he needed. The task was to make it physically available.

People like Ruburt translated inner knowledge in many ways — through acting it out, through singing or dancing, through drawing images on cave walls. It was the intellect's job to put such information to practical use, and thus the intuitions and the intellect worked hand in hand. *(Long pause.)* Man dealt then with spontaneous knowing in a more direct fashion.

(Pause at 9:10.) It is very difficult to try to explain the various

shadings of psychology that were involved. Early man did act in a more spontaneous manner, more automatically, in your terms, but not mindlessly. If you remember the early portions of our latest book *(Mass Events)*, then this information should fall into place, for consciousness emerged from the inside outward. Animals enjoy drama, and in their fashions they playact.

It was left to man to translate his inner information with a free hand. He is able to form many different kinds of cultures, for example. He puts his sciences and religions, his languages, together in multitudinous ways, but there must always be a translation of inner information outward to the world of sense. There still is. Man's capacities have not dimmed in that regard. Thinking, for example, is as automatic as ever *(amused)*. It is simply that your culture puts the various elements together in ways that stress the qualities of what you refer to as rational thinking.

When the species needs certain abilities, they rise to the fore, as in the case of Ruburt now. When you are painting pictures you are also translating inner knowledge. Early artists drew pictures to share the images they saw in their dreams. In a fashion they practiced dreaming in their sleep, and thus learned also to think (underlined) in terms of the measurement of physical images, and to move objects around in their minds before they did so physically.

Poetry was an art and a science. It conveyed quite necessary information about man and the universe. The same can be said of many cave drawings. What you had — what you still have, though you are not nearly as aware of it — was an excellent give-and-take between the inner and outer senses. Through chanting, dancing, playacting, painting, story-telling, man spontaneously translated inner sense data into physical actualization. The physical senses only present you with clues as to your own sensitivities.

Ruburt translates what I give him without being consciously aware of receiving the material in usual terms, or of translating it. It has to be broken down, particularly to a time frame, and then into concepts that can take advantage of the world view that is held in your culture. Everything must be slanted to fit the viewpoint of creatures who believe most firmly in the superiority of matter over mind — who are immersed in a particular biological framework.

(9:27.) I cannot ignore those belief structures *(intently)* — or what I say would literally be incomprehensible. All of this is automatically taken care of.

(Long pause.) Now: The species has multitudinous abilities, each necessary, each adding to the entire fulfillment and attributes of your people. Some individuals choose to specialize, following specific lines of abilities throughout many existences — accommodating these, however, to the times in which they are born. Both of you have been speakers in that regard. The methods may change. You may "speak" through art or music, through trance activities, but you will specialize in the use of the inner senses, and in translating the inner knowledge of the species, bringing it to whatever level of ordinary consciousness that is considered the official one.

(Long pause at 9:35.) You know what sound is, yet as Ruburt knows, what you consider sound is only one of sound's many spectrums. Beside translating inner images into paintings, for example, you may unknowingly be translating sensually invisible sounds into images. In a way quite impossible to describe, it would be true to say that our sessions actually translate multidimensional images into words. You have no words for the kinds of images I am speaking of, for they are not objects, nor pictures of

objects, nor images of images, but instead the inner dimensions, each separate and glowing, but connected, prisms of knowledge, that have within themselves more reality than you can presently begin to imagine.

To a certain extent, I must travel from those realities into your comprehension, wrest myself free in order to form an ever-changing, ever-moving, ever-on-the-move entity that can speak here and be there at the same time. So I am distant and close at once. That distance from you also represents the reaches, however, of the human psyche, and the vast corridors of psychological activity from which it is formed, and from which your world emerges.

For the worlds are so composed that each one is a part of each other one, and there is no disconnecting. There is no place or space, psychological, psychic, where those worlds exist apart from each other, so you cannot say that one is more highly evolved than another.

(Long pause at 9:45.) There are as many frontiers as there ever were, and there is no catastrophe that will annihilate consciousness, or put an end to earthly life. When you think in terms of earth's destruction, or the ending of the world, you are thinking of course of a continuum of time, and of beginnings and endings. From your viewpoint in space and time, it seems that planets have come and gone, stars collapsed, and when you look outward into space, it appears (underlined) that you look backward into time. (Long pause.) There are great pulsations, however, in existence — pulsations that have nothing to do with time as you understand it, but with intensities.

In the deepest of terms, the world always was and always will be. It changes its patterns of activity, it comes and goes, but it is always itself in its comings and goings. To me, that is exceedingly simple — but as far as your concepts are concerned, it can seem to imply irreconcilable complications.

End of session. A small note to our friend — again — to trust the great power of the universe that forms his own image, to trust his spontaneity, and his body's natural urges toward relaxation, motion, and creativity, as these show themselves in their own rhythms.

A dear and cozy good evening to you in your sweet house — with *(amused)* the baseball game ahead of you, and all of the loving paraphernalia that is so specific in your space and time.

("Thank you, Seth. Good night."

(9:56 P.M. "Boy, I was out with that," Jane said. "That really hits me: you can tell you're out there so far, with all of this energy, but you can't go any further, you know what I mean? At the same time, it's so simple. . . . It was a different session in some way. My feelings are that I was different, although I don't know about what different things you might get down. Right now I'm looking at the clock — and it seems that you were so far away that it seems I should take four hours to get back. Not that I had any sense of time in the session. . . ."

(The session is indeed an excellent one, and Jane's delivery, after a slow start, had often been intent and inspired.)

NOTE: SESSION OF OCTOBER 15, 1980

1. Jane called her book of poetry *If We Live Again: Or, Public Magic and Private Love*, and Prentice-Hall published it in 1982.

Poetry was her first, childhood love, and it remained a powerful creative factor throughout her life. Indeed, in some of her earliest poetry we found concepts that Seth was to elaborate upon many years later. As Seth told us in 1979, Jane had been a poet *all* of the time, in its most profound meaning. She'd been letting *If We Live Again* grow for some time as she selected poems for it from the many she had written, and kept writing.

Jane also wrote three introductory essays for the book. Here are her opening lines from the first essay, "Poetry and the Magical Approach to Life":

"To me at least, poetry — like love — implies a magical approach to life, quite different from the presently accepted rational way of looking at the world. That is, poetry brings out life's hidden nuances. It delights in forming correspondences between events that seem quite separate to the intellectually-tuned consciousness alone, and reveals undercurrents of usually-concealed actions that we quite ignore when we're most concerned about thinking rationally. Actually, that kind of vision contains its own spontaneous rationality, and often supplies us with answers more satisfying than purely intellectual ones."

APPENDIX A

THREE OF JANE'S ADVENTURES IN PREDICTION.
SETH COMMENTS. JANE'S CONTENTS OF THE MIND.

This appendix contains three of Jane Roberts' (unfinished) essays on different kinds of "prediction" and precognition experience. Also included is one excerpt by Seth about Jane's talents with a similar kind of experience.

Jane discusses "prediction" and precognition in her books: *How to Develop Your ESP Power, Adventures in Consciousness, Psychic Politics,* and *The God of Jane.*

She wrote these essays in 1980 and 1981. They were taken from her journals and edited as little as possible to preserve her original spirit. Jane usually wrote several drafts for her "own" books, but spoke her books by Seth in final draft form.

(May 1980) This small incident fascinated me.

Wednesday night after the Seth session, before bed, I suddenly began to wonder if the paintings Rob had sold to Lib's Supper Club, back in the 60s, were still there.

Rob and I started talking about them as I sat on the bed, and we got ready to retire. I remembered and described three of them, thought there was a fourth, but couldn't remember it. This is the first time we've discussed those paintings in . . . ten years?

I completely forgot our discussion until last night, Friday, when the Gallaghers [our dear friends, Peg and Bill] visited. In a lull of conversation, Peg G. leaned forward and said: "I was at Lib's Supper Club, and your paintings are still there," or other words to that effect, mentioning both Lib's and the paintings.

I felt a small sense of shock. My eyes leapt to Rob's — I could see he felt the same way. Then Peg told us that Wednesday evening, though earlier than (Rob's and my) discussion, she'd asked someone to check the signature, and saw that they were indeed Rob's.

This is the first time since the sixties that the Gallaghers have ever mentioned those paintings to us also; although they've been to Lib's many times in those years . . . It's also interesting that Peg didn't see the fourth painting, either . . . She and I seem to "pick up" from each other fairly well, according to past instances . . .

If she hadn't mentioned her visit to Lib's, and the paintings, Rob and I never would have realized that anything beyond usual perception was operating in our little discussion. And the discussion was . . . extremely clear in my mind.

So how many times does this kind of thing happen? What cross-currents of perception operate? What kinds of data do we pick up on — and why?

Rob and I can't be sure whether our discussion was Wednesday or Tuesday night. Wednesday was the night Peg G. visited Lib's, and saw the paintings.

If our discussion actually happened Tuesday, before Peg's visit (which was planned ahead of time), then we run into other possibilities than if our discussion was on Wednesday . . . (as we thought).

On Wednesday I must have picked up on Peg's visit earlier that same evening; her visit to Lib's, her specific interest in the paintings. She asked someone to check the name because she wasn't sure they were Rob's work. Then later that night, relaxed, sitting on the bed, somehow those inner perceptions (of mine) would have surfaced . . . but without revealing their source. I can't remember why I began the discussion, for example. So exactly what unconscious processing went on?

Why didn't Rob pick up the inner information and begin the discussion instead of me, since they're his paintings? And how many times do we do this, invisibly winding such data into the fabric of our perceptions, reacting to it without even realizing it?

If Rob and I discussed it on Tuesday, I could have picked up on Peg's plan to go to Lib's, wondered about Rob's paintings — and have somehow gotten my question across to her. So that, visiting the next night, she was attracted to the paintings, answering my question Friday when she gave us her account of the episode.

All of this reminds me of my old idea of a projected book: *The Contents of the Mind*, or *the Unofficial Contents of the Mind*. After reading this first page of notes about Peg G. and the paintings, I remember my old ideas . . . that we organize the contents of our minds along certain lines that then become habitual.

We're both highly interested in Rob's paintings, for instance, so of course I picked up on that kind of data from Peg. I've organized data with the focus of art in mind as a focus point through which to . . . perceive the world.

The idea is to be alert for psychological contents of the mind that we usually ignore, that science can't prove or disprove . . . where we take experience over theory.

This is another classic example of an event that science would label simply "coincidental" without being able to give any objective proof to back up its contention.

The "natural" subjective experience — the feelings involved — give the opposite explanation. They insist that more than coincidence is involved — that the event is significant.

And in such cases we have every right to go with direct experience and our feelings.

Too often *(Jane writes)* we just want to go full steam ahead — we want sublime visions. But here, in these subtle (byways) of subjective action, we very well might be seeing some of these hidden psychic motions upon which physical events rest . . . and how today's events and last year's rub against each other like leaves from the same tree. And how Seth's sessions of last August seem to apply newly to today's events. How sneaky and obvious it all is at the same time.

Today before I began work, for instance, I scribbled down ten quick phrases under the heading "Predictions: August 24, 1981." This took perhaps three minutes or so. [Presented exactly as written by Jane.]

Predictions — Monday, August 24, 1981 — Noon — Jane Roberts
1. Snow ball machine
2. Engagement once dropped re-scheduled
3. Egg carton
4. Prominent triangle — maybe gift.
5. Snow shoes?
6. Boxed-in canyon
7. Milk man
8. detective
9. Stove comes earlier.
10. double digit series

Around 1:00 P.M., as Rob and I finished lunch in the kitchen and waited for the mailman, a fan turned up. A young lad who usually showed up once a year. He was the one I described in *The God of Jane* who felt himself to be a woman trapped in a man's body. He has some suicidal tendencies, and I've worried about that. But here he was, all grins this time . . . alive and several pounds more substantial.

Rob had to go to the bank, so he excused himself and left just after the mailman arrived. I read the mail over. This year's cool August air blew through the house, and I tightened my sweater. One letter in particular caught my eyes because it was from an old friend, Ed, the man who had introduced Rob and I to begin with; a man who we had lost touch with until two years ago when he'd suddenly written from Alaska.

So as I listened to our visitor (I'll call him Larry) talk, I browsed through the letter. My thoughts went back to the years when Ed and Rob produced the detective comic strip Mike Hammer together with Micky Spillane. Then I thought of Ed's first letter of two years ago, breaking a twenty-year-old silence, mailed from Alaska where Ed was skiing. In fact, the letter before me mentioned the Alaskan ski trip. That might have been the reference that suddenly gave me small shivers.

Larry was telling me that he had a new job, running the cash register at a convenient grocery store, and I nodded but the (shivery) feeling persisted till the next moment when I checked my predictions.

Some now made perfect sense. I circled numbers 1, 5 and 8 (see prediction listing) which read: "Snow ball machine, snowshoes, detective." Surely they all applied to Ed's letter in which he mentioned his Alaskan ski trip, and friends he had when he and Rob did the detective comic strip.

The letter itself had been in the mailman's truck when I made my morning's predictions.

The predictions weren't the greatest, but they had a satisfying feel. I figured that "snow ball machine" and "snow shoes" were my interpretations to describe any snow equipment. Besides skiing Ed probably used a snowmobile and snowshoes. So I granted them as fair-enough predictions, particularly in summertime when normal associations didn't usually involve snow. I also granted a "fair" prediction to "detective."

My eyes scanned the list. Could 3 and 7 — egg carton and milk man — apply to Larry's grocery store job? These I just marked evocative. Then I thought of another connection with "milk man" — our young fan, Larry, once would only drink milk, he was on a natural food diet — or had been. In fact, I had offered him milk as I went over my predictions . . . I suddenly remembered something else. That morning before beginning work, I sat at my desk unaccountably thinking about the way Rob and I had met. I had the impulse, for no particular reason, to write about the meeting today instead of writing on this book (*The Magical Approach*) and spent a good ten minutes thinking about the entire affair. In memory's quick vivid images I saw the very first meeting:

Spring night; my first husband and I just pulled up in front of my mother's house; the rushing sounds of a car pulling in ahead of us. Ed Robinson's voice — the Ed of the Alaskan letter now received thirty years later, (the Ed who was then doing the detective comic strip referred to in the day's predictions) and a stranger's voice.

The stranger who bent his head to our car window was Rob. Ed had recognized my husband's car and followed us, asking us to go to his house to meet his new work partner, Rob, when I was finished visiting with my mother.

All of that came to mind this morning; not that it couldn't have just been "coincidence" that later in the day I hear from Ed — after making three predictions that seemed to apply to him. But surely there is a point where feelings themselves are meanings; where the heart's evidence recognizes intuitively what the intellect must question. And I know that those memories and thoughts were connected with my later predictions and Ed's letter in the noon mail. I'd been reacting to Ed's letter before its arrival.

("Results")

1, 5: In today's mail letter from Ed Robinson — Probably our 3rd?

*Anyhow — after 20 years we heard from him in 1978 — from Alaska — skiing from Alaska Back Country — he mentions Alaska skiing today. When we knew Ed Robinson — over 20 years ago — he was doing Mike Hammer comic strip for Micky Spillane. Rob joined him and that's what he was doing when I met him (Rob).

*Note: Early A.M. I think about writing today about first meeting Rob — though I'm working on Chapter Two of Magical Approach! Surprised by the impulse — then forget it.

3, 7: Just note. Evocative but not definite enough. A fan (Larry), here from Pennsylvania, says he has a new 2nd job — in grocery chain convenient market (that sells basics — nothing fancy; eggs, milk, beer, etc.). Larry drinks only milk (at one time).

2. Note: Monday, August 24. "Floyd" said he'd be here this afternoon. After not appearing on job for days. About 12:30 he calls, can't make it — again — supposedly will come tomorrow.

The next morning, Tuesday, August 25, 1981, I scribbled down another short list of predictions. Reading them back I read "old friend, Auld Lang Syne." Not likely, I thought, just after hearing from one old friend. Remembering the Ed affair of yesterday. I thought ironically this must be old friend week.

And, in a way it was. The stove we bought this week was delivered. One of the delivery men from Sears recognized Rob and I at once as a couple he had known briefly in the sixties, when we often visited with the Maples (old friends who — again — we haven't heard from in 20 years) who he had lived downstairs from.

And a kind of ghostly elegance was added Thursday when another old friend visited and showed us color slides taken in London on Xmas/New Years, 1980, and mentioned they all chimed in to sing "Auld Lang Syne."

I get the feeling that events are getting knocked into and out of prominence all the time! But catching the motion is something else again. [Presented exactly as written by Jane.]

"Predictions" — August 25, 1981 — Noon— Jane Roberts
1. Steam shovel
2. More from Dick, David
3. French Frank — Franque?
4. Silver pennent or chain
5. Fishery
6.* Old Friend, Auld Lang Syne
7. Hoe
8. night — splendor
9. Hope — name
10. Over-achiever and father

"Results"

*6 Not bad. The man who delivered our new stove from Sears turns out (today) to know us from 20 years ago. He says he lived downstairs from our old friends, Atalie and Lydia Maple who moved away in the mid-1960's.

*6 Another old friend visits August 27th, Thursday. He shows slides of a trip. Mentions they all chimed in to sing Auld Lang Syne! (New Year's last.)

Seth describes another sort of prediction experience of Jane's in Volume II of *Dreams, "Evolution" and Value Fulfillment.* From the 932nd session, which she held on August 4, 1981:

". . . One morning last weekend *(Saturday)* Ruburt [Jane] found himself suddenly and vividly thinking about some married friends. They lived out of town, separated in time by a drive of approximately (half an hour). Ruburt found himself wishing that the friends lived closer, and he was suddenly filled with a desire to see them. He imagined the couple at the house, and surprised himself by thinking that he might indeed call them later in the day and invite them down for the evening, even though she and Joseph [Rob] had both decided against guests that weekend.

Furthermore, Ruburt did not like the idea of making an invitation on such short notice. Then he became aware that those particular thoughts were intrusive, completely out of context with his immediately previous ones, for only a moment or so earlier he had been congratulating himself precisely because he had made no plans for the day or evening at all . . . about fifteen minutes later he found the same ideas returning, this time more insistently.

They lasted perhaps five minutes. Ruburt noticed them and forgot them once again. This time, however, he decided not to call his friends, and he went about his business. In about a half hour the same mental activity returned, and finding himself struck by this, he mentioned the episode to Joseph and again cast it from his mind.

By this time it was somewhat later in the day. Ruburt and Joseph ate lunch, and the mail arrived. There was a letter written the morning before *(on Friday)* by the same friends that had been so much in Ruburt's mind. They mentioned going on a trip *(on Saturday),* and specifically asked if they could visit that same afternoon. From the way the letter was written, it seemed as if the friends — call them Peter and Polly — had already started on their journey that *(Saturday)* morning, and would stop in Elmira on their return much later toward evening. There was no time to answer the letter, of course.

. . . It would be simple enough, of course, to ascribe Ruburt's thoughts and feelings to mere coincidence. He remembered the vividness of his feelings at the time, however. It looked as if Peter and Polly were indeed going to arrive almost as if Ruburt had in fact called and invited them. That evening the visit did take place. Actually, some work had prevented the couple from leaving when they intended. Instead, they called later from their home to say that they were just beginning their trip, and would stop on their way.

Ruburt was well prepared for the call by then, and for the visit . . ."

APPENDIX B

Magical Orientations and the
Motions of Probabilities.
Jane's Mental conversation

Second Essay by Jane Roberts:
Dreams for Two and Seth Begins a New Project

August 6, 1980. So we were back at the sessions again. It took me only a few seconds to come out of trance. "Though I should stay in one," I said, "because I was more comfortable than I've been all day." Because the heat didn't bother Seth, (or me speaking for him) at all. Returning to my usual state of consciousness I was instantly hot again.

"Well," Rob said, "someone said a mouthful tonight." I grinned. The crickets and wood bugs rose up in song from the summer-thick woods out back. I couldn't remember what I'd said as Seth — and I wasn't sure if I knew what magic was — or wasn't — But I knew that the night was . . . magical, alive with its own natural ceremonies. And that somehow the Seth sessions were as natural and right as the summer evening.

🌿 🌿 🌿

I began writing more and more poetry, quite caught up with many of the ideas that Seth was discussing. Actually I did a lot of scribbled poetry notes sitting on the side of the bed with the windows open and the fan full blast, trying to take my mind off the nearly steady 90-degree or higher temperature. Sometimes I thought that if Rob said it was a terrific day just one more time, I'd scream.

There were several other themes floating about our lives . . . Sue Watkins' new book *Conversations with Seth* about my E.S.P. classes was to appear in the fall. A vague uneasiness was growing in my mind: It seemed that Prentice-Hall was taking unusually long to officially clear *The God of Jane* and Seth's *The Individual and the Nature of Mass Events.* I expected to hear from my editor any day. In the meantime the pesty fleas continued their household tyranny and all of this was somehow wrapped around a ribbon of excitement as we watched the Democrats and Republicans battle on the news just before we left for our respective work rooms.

Yet all of those events seemed to happen in a slightly different kind of atmosphere than before, as Seth's ideas of the Magical Approach cast their light upon current behavior. Numerous but subtle instances of "magical" orientation kept appearing in our lives. We seemed to catch tiny glimpses of ordinary events before they were fully formed, and to sense the motions of probabilities invisibly but clearly stirring in the over-heated summer air. In the beginning these suggestive events just stretched our imaginations and thoughts, but later they became numerous and persistent so that we had to take them into consideration as we made normal decisions.

As with so many instances, these weren't esoteric startling visions, but a kind of in-between event, difficult to identify, or one like the following, that was second-handed. On August 7th at supper time a young fan appeared unexpectedly at the door. I'll call him John. Rob grinned when he saw him; John had been here twice before (once a year), he was good-humored, good-looking, eager, healthy and strong. He was engaging, and knew it. We talked to him for an hour (while, alas, dinner got cold), but he was one of those people pleasantly gifted in a variety of fields who hadn't yet settled down to concentrate on the development of any one or two abilities in particular. He was like some kid admiring a box of chocolates; each piece representing one of his own talents, wondering which piece to nibble on first. Somewhere in the conversation, with a smiling sense of wonder, he told us what had happened as he drove through Elmira on the way to our house.

As he drove into town . . . he saw on the street a girl who looked familiar. No wonder — he'd met her at a bar the first time he was in town.

"I've only been in this town twice, when I visited you before," he said. "Yet earlier tonight driving down a street I suddenly recognized a girl who looked familiar. I slowed the car and looked. She was walking on the sidewalk, and sure enough, it was the same girl I'd met at a bar during my first trip to Elmira. I could hardly believe it, but I stopped the car and we talked awhile. She remembered me at once. So the chances of that kind of meeting must be astronomical." She had told him he could stay at her place overnight. Coincidence? We only spoke to him for an hour, and he said he had wondered earlier what he'd do with the whole evening . . . so what exactly happened at the magical level of activity?

The same night I had an experience with a mental conversation [that turned out to be precognitive].[1] I think both instances represent activity and communication . . . at the magical level. They represent a kind of mobility . . . a psychological motion, at another level than the usually conscious one.

Our next scheduled Seth session was for the following Monday — another day high in the 90s, and I found myself anticipatory and hopeful: Would Seth discuss some of those issues? I felt again that an entire new "package" of session material was coming our way — and I wanted to be able to put it to practical use. See the second session, with an edited version of Rob's notes, deleting only highly personal material.

[1]See note 4 about Mary, in Session Three.

APPENDIX C

JANE AND ROB MEET A SKEPTICAL PSYCHOLOGIST AND HIS MAGIC.
JANE'S POEM: "MAGIC IS PUBLIC AS THE AIR . . ."

Gramacy was a psychologist and a magician, and he came to our house because he was a scientist looking for some real magic. He was a compact, dark-skinned and dark-haired person with soft brown large eyes that were kept half closed when he was being a psychologist, and turned larger, commanding and yet inviting when he was being a magician. Both his eyes and his hands were really too expressive for a scientist's, and he tried to be a scientist even when he was being a magician — perhaps then most of all.

He turned on a small recorder; classical music with a tinny quality swirled through the room. He bowed his dark head for just a moment then lifted it, those soft eyes now . . . softer and harder at the same time; his hands moved in rhythm with the music; his whole body was a marvel of motion; shoulders, head, arms, chest — his whole trunk, responding to the music. Then at his command, four silver dollars disappeared through the tabletop and he caught them underneath in the palm of his hands. Playing cards appeared and disappeared. He was in a trance of his own; so were Rob and I, watching. And in the back of his mind was the improbable hope that one day, somehow, the coins would *really* go through the tabletop. . . .

"Or that something will happen to me, that will prove that there *is* more to life than usual cause and effect," he said to us. "I almost believe that there is. But in my own life, I can't find it. It's not in my bag of tricks," he went on suggestively. "But if someone else told me things about myself that no one could know. . . ."

"Why not catch *yourself* with knowledge you're not supposed to have?" I suggested.

"Like precognitive information? I never have any. That's what I mean," he said.

I replied, "Haven't you ever known that someone was going to call you, just a moment before the party actually called on the phone? Or haven't you ever known that the doorbell would ring just before it did, or that you'd meet someone you hadn't seen in a long time just before you actually do meet?"

"Coincidence," Gramacy answered dourly. "I'd explain such instances that way."

"But if you wrote down each such instance and kept track, you might find that there were too many to assign to coincidence, or discover that coincidence couldn't apply to some at all," I said. "You'd have your own growing body of instances to examine. You can't prove that coincidence is or isn't responsible for such things, but you *could* consider the unofficial hypothesis as a possibility. You might find that you have proof of precognition in your own life that you're ignoring."

He raised a furry eyebrow: "I'd still rather have some really great event happen. I mean, why not?" He grinned. "Like the *New York Times* ad test with Seth you two did and wrote up in *The Seth Material.* Now that would convince me!"

Rob replied, "That test was just one of many we did. We didn't discount anything. When you use coincidence as a handy explanation for everything, then you never get that far."

Gramacy nodded. "I know a magician can duplicate almost any *physical* manifestation that a psychic can perform. . . ."

"That's why we don't bother with effects that can be duplicated," Seth suddenly said, "but with this performance and our books, which cannot be duplicated. For where does the material in the books come from? Where does it keep coming from?"

"Uh," Gramacy said. Rob laughed. And in a twinkling I'd changed into Seth. "Look" I said, "no strings, no cards hidden within cards, no bag of tricks beside me on the floor." Smiling, hearty, Seth talked about magic and cause and effect, but at the same time he demonstrated a magic that is beyond the clever manipulation of appearances. Another personality from whatever realm had joined the party.

It's really unfortunate and quite unusual that we didn't record the session. Seth came through before I thought to remind Gramacy that he could record Seth, if Seth came through. But somehow in my mind at least, not recording that session added to it's magical quality . . . the spontaneous psychological or psychic transformation came and went . . . We were sitting at the living-room table with the lamplight clear on my face; Gramacy could follow Seth's psychological passage; see my features change, taking on ever so subtly those other contours. And Seth's voice was jovial, booming, you didn't have to strain to hear those words. There was no prepared message either. We hadn't known that Gramacy was a scientist until he told us that night, and it was as a magician rather than as a scientist that Seth addressed him, telling him to trust his dramatic and imaginative flair.

Magic is public
as the air,
so obvious
and clear that it appears
invisible.
And we look through it
at the world,
which rises up about us
everywhere.

When we wake up
in the morning,
the world is always there
waiting.
We never catch it
coming or going,
and no smallest part of it
disappears
before our eyes,
but stays intact.

But all of that implies
just too much
precision
to happen all by
itself,
a whole world mysteriously
appearing
out of nowhere,
putting itself together
just right
without instructions
or previous experience.

Such a masterly
production

makes me think instead
that
there are
clues
we've overlooked.

We like to think
that chance alone
collected the pieces of
the world,
stitching together the
continents,
turning the dumb elements
into fish and fowl,
and you and me, finally.

Of Master Magicians
whose conjurings
feature the amazing tricks
of space and time,
produced so skillfully
and fast
that we're dazzled with
the effects,
and miss the magical
slights of hand
beneath
the flashy gestures
of the days and nights.

Producing
from it's magical bag
of tricks,
one marvelous form
of life after another,
fish,

bird,
monkey,
man
(not just one dove
or rabbit)
with a skill and swiftness
so astute
that our wise men think
one turns into the other!

Juggling a
million million
atoms
all at once,
spinning them into
twirling cells of men
and whales,
tricky,
spinning solid mountains
from thin air,
with fish transformed
into flying birds —

Now *that's* A Magic Show!

Jane Roberts
August 29, 1980

APPENDIX D

JANE'S CHALLENGES WITH HER SCOPE OF IDENTITY VS.
THE SCIENTIFIC COMMUNITY

As her psychic abilities began to rapidly grow, following her initiation of the Seth material late in 1963, Jane couldn't help but become more and more concerned about consciously enlarging her "scope of identity." It became obvious to us later, of course, that even her first doubts and questions about things psychic made it inevitable that she would confront such a basic issue. As was characteristic of us, also, we worked by ourselves for a long time as we attempted to learn more about what we were doing. But naive creatures that we were, when we did begin to reach out we were quite unprepared for the skepticism we would meet from the learned "establishment." In large part, that rejection was to continue. Very understandable, then, that Jane, both for herself and for Seth, would write so eloquently about the disparity between her psychic abilities and "the currently scientifically-oriented blend of rationalism," as Seth describes that quality earlier in this Session Six for *The Magical Approach.*

Ever since she began studying Jane's work fourteen years ago, my companion, Laurel Lee Davies, has been very conscious of the conflict between the rationalistic dominance so common in our culture, and the potential for greater development that she sensed within herself. As she researched Jane's published and unpublished notes, journals, and books for *The Magical Approach*, Laurel learned that my wife had originally intended to call this book *The Magical Approach: A Jane/Seth Book*, and wrote of it as being "a psychic-naturalistic journal." If Jane had planned to add to Seth's original sessions, what might she have included? We found several of her relevant essays, and have presented them in these appendices and in her Introduction. Laurel pointed out a number of forceful passages Jane wrote on cultural acceptance in *The God of Jane* in 1980 — the same year in which she dictated *The Magical Approach* for Seth. (Prentice-Hall published *The God of Jane* in 1981.)

For example, in Chapter 12 of her own book, Jane began an impassioned four-page discussion of the subject by quoting her own notes:

Science worships skepticism, unless skepticism is applied to science, its hypotheses, procedures, or methods. What we need are more skeptics who are not afraid to judge the claims of science with the same fine discrimination used to examine other alternate disciplines and fields of endeavor. Like *The New York Times*, science publishes "all the news that's fit to print," meaning all of the news that fits into the officially-accepted view of reality. That news is already invisibly censored, and yet we're supposed to live our lives in accordance with that official definition of experience.

Inspired by Jane's ideas, Laurel wrote on September 27, 1994:

Science arose out of a religious world that was filled with "witchcraft." It began as a protection from, and a defense against, some of the mysteries of the natural world. It has since found itself denying the realities it arose to tame.

Jane Roberts and Robert Butts have had letters from scientists of all kinds, many of them academics. In some ways the Seth material has been given credit by the establishment; being taught as university course work, for example. But often readers have been afraid to admit publicly that they have found truth in metaphysical sources. They have been trapped by the boundaries of what science has so far accepted into its family: an ethnocentrically perfect "set" of beliefs, with metaphysical mysteries denied, avoided, or written out.

So far, metaphysics has only been entertainment, a step-science of our culture; part of the extended family of science for the purposes of inspiration and ideas, but not given credit as scientific truth. Frowned upon. Even feared.

Scientific truths have always been rewritten through the centuries. I believe that metaphysics is a science of empathetic responses.

The Magical Approach is a perfect example of a scientifically-unacceptable method of working with reality. Yet, The Magical Approach works. I can state that with amazement from my own experience. At first it may not seem to be giving you the results you expect, but you are working within spacious time. Your schedule may have to change. You may start bringing in different experiences than you think you are seeking, then materialize your original requirements later on. Your wish-focus disappears into Frameworks 2, 3, and 4,[1] and then reappears later. Natural magic: This process can bring you more complex ideas and proof than you conceived of.

The complexity of life and reality encompasses both positive and not-so-positive experiences within value fulfillment. The Magical Approach can help with both. I will be interested in hearing about your magical research.

It is an honor for me to have worked as a research and editorial assistant for this book. I have absolute faith that Seth and Jane Roberts, as well as Rob, know how I mean that with all my heart.

Laurel Davies

---

[1] Rob describes Framework 2 in Session One, Footnote 2. Seth discusses Frameworks 3 and 4 in *The Individual and the Nature of Mass Events* as creative environments to keep in mind also.

ABOUT THE AUTHOR

Jane Roberts (May 8, 1929 – September 5, 1984) grew up in Saratoga Springs, New York where she attended Skidmore College. She was a prolific writer in a variety of genres including poetry, short stories, children's literature, and fiction when in 1963 she began to receive messages from a non-physical energy personality who called himself "Seth." Her husband, Robert F. Butts, an artist and writer, recorded the messages and together they dedicated their lives to the publication of Seth's teachings.

Jane's international bestselling "Seth Books" include *Seth Speaks, The Nature of Personal Reality, The Nature of the Psyche, The Individual and the Nature of Mass Events, The "Unknown" Reality, Dreams "Evolution" and Value Fulfillment,* and *The Magical Approach.* Her enormously popular novels include *The Education of Oversoul Seven, The Further Education of Oversoul Seven,* and *Oversoul Seven and the Museum of Time* (now published as *The Oversoul Seven Trilogy*).

The Seth Books are world-renowned for comprising one of the most profound bodies of work ever written on the true nature of reality. They have become classics in the fields of psychology and personal growth, and stand out as one of the major forces that led to the New Age philosophical movement in the 1970s.

Today, Yale University Library maintains a collection of Jane's writings, journals, poetry, audio and video recordings, correspondence, and other materials (the "Jane Roberts Papers") donated by her husband and other individuals.

New Seth Books, Online Seth Courses, Seth Conferences & Workshops

"The Early Sessions" – by Jane Roberts

"The Early Sessions" are the first 510 sessions dictated by Seth during the first six years of his relationship with Jane Roberts and her husband, Robert F. Butts. Published in nine volumes, these new Seth books offer fresh insights from Seth on a vast array of topics.

"The Personal Sessions" – by Jane Roberts

"The Personal Sessions," originally referred to as "the deleted sessions," are Seth-dictated sessions that Jane Roberts and Robert F. Butts considered to be of a highly personal nature, and therefore kept separate from the main body of the Seth material.

The Seth Audio Collection

These audios consist of rare recordings of Seth speaking through Jane Roberts during her classes in Elmira, New York in the 1970s, and recorded by her student, Rick Stack. This collection represents the best of Seth's comments gleaned from over 120 class sessions.

Online Seth Courses

This in-home learning experience offers an intensive immersion into some of the most important concepts presented in the Seth material. (Includes live online interactive webinars with instructor Rick Stack.)

Seth Conferences & Workshops

These gatherings offer a unique opportunity to meet people of like mind, increase your understanding of both inner and outer reality, and enhance your ability to create your ideal life.

For further information, contact New Awareness Network, Inc.
(516) 869-9108 between 9:00 A.M. – 5:00 P.M. ET
sumari@sethcenter.com, or visit our websites:
www.sethcenter.com
www.sethlearningcenter.org
www.sethconference.org

ALSO FROM AMBER-ALLEN PUBLISHING

Seth Speaks by Jane Roberts. In this essential guide to conscious living, Seth clearly and powerfully articulates the concept that we create our own reality according to our beliefs.

The Nature of Personal Reality by Jane Roberts. Seth explains how the conscious mind directs unconscious activity, and has at its command all the powers of the inner self.

The Nature of the Psyche by Jane Roberts. Seth reveals a startling new concept of self, answering questions about many aspects of the psyche, including love, dreams, sexuality, and death.

The Individual and the Nature of Mass Events by Jane Roberts. Extending the idea that we create our own reality, Seth explores the connection between personal beliefs and world events.

The "Unknown" Reality, Volumes One and Two by Jane Roberts. Exploring the interdependence of multiple selves, Seth explains how understanding unknown dimensions can change the world as we know it.

Dreams, "Evolution," and Value Fulfillment, Volumes One and Two by Jane Roberts. These books answer crucial questions about the entire significance of Seth's system of thought, as he takes us on an odyssey to identify the origins of our universe and our species.

The Oversoul Seven Trilogy by Jane Roberts. The adventures of Oversoul Seven are an intriguing fantasy, a mind-altering exploration of our being, and a vibrant celebration of life.

The Way Toward Health by Jane Roberts. In this final "Seth Book," Jane channels the teachings of Seth from her hospital bed as her husband shares the intimate story of her final days. Includes Seth speaking about self-healing and the mind's effect upon our physical health.

The Four Agreements by don Miguel Ruiz. A powerful code of conduct that can rapidly transform our lives to a new experience of freedom, true happiness, and love.

This book is copublished by Amber-Allen Publishing
and New World Library.

New World Library is dedicated to publishing books and
audios that help improve the quality of our lives.

For information about other fine books and audios from
New World Library, please call or visit us online.

Phone: (415) 884-2100 or (800) 972-6657
www.newworldlibrary.com

Amber-Allen Publishing is dedicated to bringing a message
of love and inspiration to all who seek a higher
purpose and meaning in life.

For information about other bestselling titles from
Amber-Allen Publishing, please call or visit us online.

Phone: (415) 499-4657 or (800) 624-8855
www.amberallen.com